Major Thompson Goes French

The new Major Thompson novel finds our Blimpish hero forsaking his heritage and opting for French citizenship, having decided that England 'has had it'. It is hilarious. *Merci*, Mr. Daninos, very much!

PIERRE DANINOS

Major Thompson Goes French

The New Notebooks of
MAJOR W. MARMADUKE THOMPSON

Translated, from the French, by
MOURA BUDBERG

W. H. ALLEN
LONDON & NEW YORK
1971

LE MAJOR TRICOLOR © ZEBRA PUBLICATIONS

ENGLISH TRANSLATION © PIERRE DANINOS 1971

THE CARTOON OF MAJOR THOMPSON IS BY WALTER GOETZ

PRINTED AND BOUND IN GREAT BRITAIN BY
THE GARDEN CITY PRESS LIMITED
LETCHWORTH, HERTFORDSHIRE
FOR THE PUBLISHERS
W. H. ALLEN & COMPANY LIMITED
ESSEX STREET, LONDON WC2R 3JG

ISBN 0 491 00216 5

CONTENTS

An open letter to the French people from Major W. Marmaduke Thompson (I.A. Retd.)

Mes chers amis français (as you would put it, and as you might wish me to put it), my publishers have put it to me that the title of this book could give rise to some perplexity. You in France have, after all, become accustomed to thinking of me as an Englishman, and indeed I have borne that appellation with modest pride for many a year. But now I have decided to become a Frenchman. Some of you at least must now be wondering what can have brought about this change of heart—this leap into reasonableness and realism? Others may equally be wondering, "What fiendish plot is he up to now?" Does he think, this perfidious hyper-Englishman, that after so many General warnings he can pull the wool over a Frenchman's eyes?

Well, there *is* in fact a leap in the offing, for Great

7

Britain is about to spring irrevocably into the welcoming arms of the Common Market. However, notwithstanding the apparent inevitability of this event, it may have occurred to you that there is less than complete agreement among my countrymen as to the desirability of becoming Common.

I have so long striven to create understanding between our two peoples, where formerly there was only *entente*, that I now feel positively duty bound to try to dispel this impression of reluctance. And what better way could there be than by placing myself in the forefront of this mighty marketward march of nations?[1]

Whatever others may have believed, I have always understood perfectly well that the key to the portals of the E.E.C. was in the gift of your country, so much so that France and the Six are as inseparable as Snow White and her dwarfs. This fact is doubly advantageous as far as I am concerned, since it both simplifies the problem of how an indivisible Major can enter a six-part Union (still by no means a unity); and also justifies my choosing, as I would naturally prefer to do, your country rather than any of the others.

Circumstances are bringing us closer all the time, of course. We are already becoming accustomed to counting our pennies in hundredths of a pound; soon our schoolchildren will be singing a song of two and a half pence, a pocket full of rye (though gloomy prophets of the effects upon our agriculture of our joining suggest that the pocket may be no more than half full); in a year or two our nursery rhyme will enquire how many kilometres to Babylon, and our advertisements

[1] *Marche vers le marché.*

8

admonish us to drinka litre milka day; though I suppose it will be too much to hope that our leather-jacketed motorcycle enthusiasts will be doing an (illegal) thousand kilos up the motorway.

And now, of course, both our countries have been baptized, some might say purged, in the fire of devaluation. We cannot but be brought together by a Common misfortune, and there are many of my countrymen who would gladly adapt your Proudhon and prudently say that 'devaluation is theft'.[2]

So here I come, by no means shirking the possibility that I may lose in the translation, willingly exchanging my tea for coffee, right-hand drive for left, and government by stealth for government by referendum. I trust that becoming French will become me, and that when I have be-come I shall be wel-come.

[2] *'Devaloriser, c'est devaliser.'*

I

THE FRANCO-FRENCH PROBLEM

I HAVE SPENT a great deal of time in, and as much thought on, your country, and as a result I tend to the opinion, as I bend from the balcony from which Foreigners notoriously observe you, that the world contains fifty million Frenchmen and some three and a half thousand million Foreigners. Either one is lucky or one is not, and I find it altogether understandable that the only country that is hexagonal, temperate and pure in heart should fill Foreigners with a sense of resentment that can drive them to the most regrettable excesses.

These were most apparent during the General's reign, when Belgians, Dutchmen and sometimes even Englishmen would take the liberty of expressing opinions on Prague or Italy without first obtaining the approval of Paris. It was clear then that the Common Market would be French or not exist at all. 'Foreign

plot', 'Foreign highhandedness', 'Foreign intrigue'—
rarely had Foreigners been in such disgrace in France.
Under the rule of your democratic monarch, the de-
nunciation of Foreigners was current coin, particularly
in financial spheres. Indeed when the approach of your
devaluation was producing a heavy run on gold, one of
your Ministers declared, "Anyone who does not love
the franc does not love France!"

What other country could unite her currency and
her people so euphoniously? Surrounded by black-
marketeers dealing in marks, roubles, pounds, dollars,
pesetas and lira, France alone has managed to give its
name to her currency. Who else can claim to be on
such affectionate terms with her coinage? She is,
furthermore, the country of franc-speaking, people are
franc as gold there, and a franc is always a franc, *je
sais*; although everyone—and particularly those
Frenchmen who keep France in their hearts and their
money in Zurich—knows that the Swiss franc is not
quite franc. Indeed, it is francly not quite playing
the game.

One can see therefore that a Frenchman who sends
his capital abroad is a detestable speculator—a
deserter, even. On the other hand a Foreigner who
decides to place his capital in France is, if your newspapers are to be trusted—making a wise investment.
Anyone who fails to understand this must be either
an idiot or a stranger to your delightful nuances. They
are, incidentally, the same nuances that I encounter
in the person of Monsieur Requillard when I go to

tennis championships with him. If a Frenchman's ball drops dead just over the net and takes a Foreigner by surprise my friend exclaims "His stop-volleys are really brilliant", while if the Foreigner brings off the same shot a few minutes later, it is "a dirty trick".

But let us get back to more serious matters. Suppose the managing director of Saint-Gobin wants to deal to his counterpart at Boussois a lethal blow and put him out of business? All he has to do is to go on television and reveal that six out of ten of the latter's directors are *Foreigners*. This blemish in their birth can never be forgiven. But if the French are majority shareholders in a Brazilian or Mexican company, this is the fruit of a generous policy of expansion which is an integral part of France's unselfishness. Besides, can one call a Frenchman a Foreigner? He is first and foremost a Frenchman—a Frenchman is never Foreign. A Foreigner, on the other hand, always has the opportunity of becoming French.

This is not only because every man has two countries, etc., etc., but also, and mainly, because your country, despite all appearances, is not a xenophobe for nothing (though a cool hundred million would be, as you say, another pair of sleeves). No country is readier to honour deserving Foreigners and give them a chance to become French. Particularly if they run faster than other people, hurl themselves down ski-slopes more rapidly and keep goal better.

At the time of the last Presidential election Monsieur Poher, the interim President of the Republic (remember him?), was obliged to defend himself from his critics by saying, "It is possible to be a patriot and yet have friends abroad".

You have to be a dirty Foreigner, a *rosbif* and irrevocably damned to utter such lunacies; or to dare to say, for instance, that the French regard the universe as an enormous, ill-defined circle with Paris at its centre. I beg your pardon, it was a Frenchman who wrote that—one Henri Bidou, in the '30s. You can't trust anyone these days. All the same, it's better to rely on someone who was born at Givet than on a fellow like Curtius, who was unlucky enough to be born a German but prevented one feeling sorry for him by having the cheek to write "Abroad, the provinces and Paris still represent to the French the planet's three concentric zones". He must have bitten M. Bidou.

Even today, the tenant of the Elysée, though prepared to admit Europe into France, is at pains to make it clear that, "The idea itself of Europe must be freed from dreams and lack of restraint".

I gather, with the help of my translator, that this statement refers to supranationality, which is considered to be a vice and possibly even a conspiracy. I must reluctantly confess that the thought of those dreams set me dreaming too. The Burgundian of say 1469 who allowed his imagination to roam so far that he supposed the day might come when he would be able to go to Paris without a passport—either because France had become Burgundian or because Paris had annexed Dijon—must have cherished the same chimera. But only an Englishman's warped mentality would maintain that France owes her unity to a series of plots that caused the Dukedoms and Kingdoms of Aquitaine, Burgundy and Savoy to fall under one central control.

Europe is not France and, if Europeans have created a United States elsewhere than in Europe, everyone knows that that is a barbarous country, only worth a rare visit. One wonders how you have even allowed the people of Stockholm and Rome to use the same No Parking signs as your own. When I think that Denaïnos is naive enough to regard this as a sign of progress and a first timid step towards a federal system, I would like to give him a parking ticket. But no, I will just leave him to his fancies and enjoy M. Pompidou's recent words. I was very sad when your General put us into quarantine, like a ship anchored off your coast, so how could I fail to be delighted now that we have received permission at last to weigh anchor and come closer to you?

With the rest of the world isolated, and Foreigners brushed aside, there only remains France and the French. If, as the title of one of your films suggests, God Chose Paris (it would have been interesting to see the faces of the French if that cinematic God had chosen New York—or London, for that matter, so long as I am not there), then all we can do with Paris, France, and the French—even if they are M. Pompidou, M. Chaban-Delmas[1] and the General's shade all

[1] M. Chaban-Delmas has been Prime Minister since M. Pompidou's election as President.

joined together—is grin and bear them. Which is by no means easy. I don't mind telling you.

Certain shallow-minded 'experts', who have plenty of time to waste and are employed by Foreigners—or as specialists in foreign policy, anyway—are constantly talking about the Franco-German problem, the Franco-American problem and Franco-British prospects (I would not be so bold as to write Anglo-French or Germano-French!).

When I stop to consider the fierce opposition that General de Gaulle came up against and that M. Pompidou and M. Chaban-Delmas are meeting today, it is clear to me that France's Number One problem is the Franco-French one. And it is equally clear that this outstanding nation, which has for centuries held aloft the torch of civilization, is far from meanly contemplating a European Federation or a United States of Europe (the only existing United States are better left where they are), and has disclaimed all responsibility for these dubious manoeuvres from the start in order to devote herself generously to herself. There is enough there to keep everyone busy.

How, indeed, do you govern a country where the employers abuse the State, the workers the employers, the upper middle classes the trade unions; where the peasants are against the communists, the communists against the socialists, the socialists against the maoists, the psychiatrists against the psychoanalysts, the pedestrians against the motorists, the motorists against the police, the walkers against the *boule*-players, the clergy against the pill-takers; where children devour teachers, students devour their professors, ministers devour each other, and where, since no one admits to belonging to the right, the left is reduced to abusing those of its leftists who accuse it of conservatism? Your young and dynamic President of the Council, for whom my translator has considerable respect tennis-wise, because Chaban-Delmas can beat him hollow *à plates coutures,* (as you would say—what coutures are these?), said quite recently, "It is vital that Frenchmen should not make life intolerable for each other".

All the more so since they still have such a good life. Even the least fortunate amongst you still enjoy, at the time of writing, the most precious of all privileges —one which no longer exists in Moscow or Peking or Athens or Lhasa or La Paz or Lima—liberty of thought, of speech and of unrestricted travel. Can it be true that the French only appreciate liberty when they have been deprived of it? History would seem to say so. Deny it, my dear friends, you gentle, vicious people, deny it! If Europe is summed up for you by what Gobineau said of the Republic ("No one wants it, but everyone clings to it")—so be it! But may I hope that while you still have everything that makes for happiness, you will not, just because you enjoy so many liberties, fall into the hands of a leader, this time not even a providential General but some NCO or other, who would come to restore law and order in the name of democracy.

Has not your Latin sister, seeking to work this almost worn out vein, found good souls prepared to plunge her once again into the delights of fascism, on masquerading as general disorders? What does it matter whether totalitarian police régimes belong to the right or the left? In either case, the citizens pay the bill, and the service is not *tout compris*—thinking costs extra.

II

HOW TO BECOME FRENCH

 DURING HIS REIGN, which although he has left the throne is by no means over and will doubtless continue long after he has gone, General de Gaulle put the whole thing very clearly. The great *mutation*[1], on which our entry into the Common Market depends, must spring, not from negotiations, but from the actions and will of the *'grand peuple anglais'*.[2] Consequently, although I am an infinitesimal fraction of a whole which is itself now reduced to so little, I have decided to apply myself to becoming if not a European, at least a Frenchman.

Some people, including no doubt many of my fellow countrymen, will be shocked that one of Her Gracious

[1] This word is all the rage nowadays, and shows how much your country has—may I say—'changed' during my absence.

[2] I have put this phrase in French since one no longer dares to write it in English.

Majesty's subjects, grown old in her service, should make such a decision. Growing old is forgivable, but to go and commit treason at my age—well, the good Lord will be my witness. I am setting about this startling metamorphosis in the same disinterested spirit as your General—for the common good, and the Market of the same name.

And, *'Grand Dieux'*[3] when a scion of the poor old lion tries to turn himself into a cock, albeit a cock which has itself lost many of its glorious feathers though it still bears itself with Gaullist pride, surely this is a sort of blasted *mutation?* Not of major importance *bien sûr*—that is a French prerogative—but quite big enough for us.

While no moment is propitious for so rash an undertaking, the present difficulties and needs make it easier for me to face it. As a retired Indian Army Major, I am quite astounded by the goings-on both in the head office of the Empire and in its former branches. But what is happening elsewhere is just as distressing to us. Our influence used to be world wide, but now we have shut down. Like landowners who can no longer afford to keep up their country seats, we have retired to one of the wings, soon we shall be reduced to begging at the gatehouse without any certainty of ever gaining admission.

Born in an Empire on which the sun never set, I find it very painful to be condemned to live in a small island above which—I can assure you—it never rises. This is a terrible comedown for the proud lion, when India, Egypt, the Sudan have been wrenched away,

[3] 'Good heavens!'

and only Fiji and Saint Helena remain in its feeble claws . . . ! A little island, that is all we are! If your General had not been there to remind us that we are a great nation, no one would give it a thought. But I give it a thought. I belong to that rapidly vanishing species of mankind that cannot read in a newspaper, 'Withdrawal of British troops east of Suez speeded up', without the blood freezing in their veins—as you say in that logical language of yours to indicate that the matter does *not* leave you cold.

Not only are we nowhere any more, we also no longer know where to go. We have withdrawn from Zanzibar, we are about to withdraw from Singapore and our towns swarm with Puerto Ricans, Indians, Guineans, Malays and Maltese so that I sometimes wonder whether there is going to be a single corner left for us to hide. What a disaster for a Major, even a retired one! Some nights my Imperial nightmares become so bad that I see the sea sweeping over our whole island and, apart from myself, no one left to sink with dignity beneath the waves, colours flying in the best Naval tradition, except a handful of effemin-ate adolescents.

You, too, I know, have had to abandon the finest ornaments of your irksome empire. But at least you still have a noble voice to remind you constantly of your greatness and to soothe you with that caressing word which our governments would prefer to elimin-ate from our vocabulary. And you still know what you are, because the General himself has told you: '*la France sera toujours la France*!'

But we don't know what we are any more.

Since the General, who continues to think of us as a boat moored off your shores, has decreed it, we are not Europeans—even though we are anchored only a few minutes away. Despite our natural inclination to allow ourselves—I am quoting the General still—to be swept by the currents towards the open sea, and despite the allegations of those who look on us as the star-spangled banner's 51st State, we are definitely not Americans. The theory that our regular absorption of China tea and Kenya coffee beans should eventually make us Afro-Asians is not generally accepted. Thus it is in distressing uncertainty as to who I am that I have decided to become what I never was.

I could of course have tried to become a citizen of a United Europe. But since it is France which has shown the greatest zeal—I would say 'tenacity' if you had not reserved that word for us—in keeping the door to Europe closed against us and, since we have so many French friends who had no hesitation in taking up long and glorious residence with us—bed, board and laundry—during the war, when they found us very acceptable partners, it is logical that I should begin, or rather pursue, my initiation with your country.

Oh, how I long to be a Frenchman!

But I am setting myself a hard goal in trying to be a Gaul. For an Englishman, it amounts to squaring the circle; the circle in this case being a club limited to six members.

Furthermore, unless one is a chameleon, how can one, in the course of half a century, be in turn true-

blue and *populaire* red, germanophobe and germano-
phile, anglophile and anglophobe, Pétainist and Gaullist, americanophile and americanophobe, last-ditcher
and capitulator, colonialist and emancipator, Viet-
bashcr and friend of Chairman Mao? And, having
achieved this, how can one assert in all good faith that
Italians are fickle, Englishmen irresolute and Russians
always ready to change sides? How can one ardently
kiss the 'armoured cars of Liberation' and burn the
colours that, only a short time before, one was burning to see arrive? In short, how can one be like M.
Requillard, who dropped in on me one morning mut-
tering, "Everyone has two countries, his own and
France", and that same evening went up to the Etoile
to shout, "France for the French!"?

At first sight it seems a hopeless undertaking.

All the same, I am going to take a chance. Ready?
Play! Or, as you so elegantly put it on TV, *"Top,
c'est parti!"*

The best proof that it is not easy to be French is
the fact that the French themselves do not always
manage it.

When the first Frenchman remarks to one of his
interviewers that the French are cattle and speaks
of *France vacharde*,[4] it is quite clear that, despite the
importance he accords to the agricultural calling, this
herd only *vaguement* (the French half of my son
would say *vachement*) corresponds to the particular

[4] If the eminent commentator J.-R. Tournoux is to be
believed, the General said, "The French are cattle, France is
a country of cattle". The quotation appears several times in
La Tragédie du Général.

23

image of France that the General has always harboured.

There are, then, Frenchmen and Frenchmen. What matters is to distinguish between the cattle and the genuine ones.

Exactly how many of the latter are there among the fifty million? The General was returned to power by only 54 per cent of the voters; should I conclude, as ill-disposed people have done, that there is slightly less than an even chance that any Frenchman I pass in the street is not a genuine one? Certainly not. That would be ridiculous.

But let me descend from the General to the particular and pay a call on my friends the Quincharts. I once lost my way when trying to find their house in the country, some twenty-five miles from Paris, I asked a young farm worker the way.

"Quinchart," he said "Quinchart. . . . Do you know any Quincharts?" he asked another countryman, who must have been his father.

"Ah, yes. . . . They're the foreigners who came to live at the foot of the hill on the other side of the river, about six months ago."

"I'm afraid," I said, as we always say without a trace of fear, "that you must be mistaken. M. Quincart is French and so is his wife."

"They're Parisians. That's the same thing as far as we're concerned. They aren't from these parts, are they?"

Again, take M. de Stumpf-Quichelier, the chairman and managing director of an important company. It is evident that he is living abroad in France, for he never stops complaining about people who do not speak the same language and who have to have absolutely everything explained to them.

"But what about your right-hand man, M. X?" I ask.

"A Lyonnais! You know what I mean?"

"And the technical director?"

"An idiot!"

"Well, the head of the publicity department?"

"Useless!"

"And all those young men just out of college?"

"Inefficient and conceited!"

All of which leaves me with the distressing impression that M. de Stumpf-Quichelier is condemned to live in a country of fifty million people of whom all but one are hopelessly inefficient. How France can contain so many millions of halfwits and still be the most intelligent country in the world completely baffles me—but we English can be very dense. Whether we are concerned with M. de Stumpf-Quichelier or someone else, it is quite clear that the true Frenchman —that is, the one you happen to be talking to at the time—is surrounded by scoundrels, spivs, cheats, schemers and dimwits, all of them usurpers of, among other things, the title of 'Frenchman'. Which explains why one of this rich country's most popular refrains is 'Poor France!'.

The unhappiness in this beautiful country, which wants only to be happy, springs from the fact that although it is envied by foreigners for its famous gaiety, by Northern and Tropical peoples for its matchless geographical position, by lesser fry who lack any definite shape for its model hexagonality, by the dress-makers of London and New York for its innate elegance, and by the whole world for its wine, its three hundred and fifty cheeses, its women, its coast and its countryside, it is at the same time inhabited by fifty million citizens who are unworthy of it—except for whoever happens to be speaking to you at the time. His cry of 'Poor France!' implies that if only all the other Frenchmen were like him things would be a great deal better.

That this exceptional country of exceptions is amply proved by the ease with which one comes across them. Not only is it undeniable that the man at the head of it was exceptional, but exceptions roam the streets and, even more, the highways.

My friend and translator must have driven me down to his country house a hundred times—perhaps two hundred. And (hang me if it's not the gospel truth) we have *never* slowed down for the signs saying 60 . . . 50 . . . 40 . . . in that nice little tunnel that leads to your great *autoroute du sud,* without being passed by two, five, even ten other cars. Foreigners? Not at all. The number plates were unmistakably French. Clearly all these exceptional drivers do not regard themselves as bound by the regulations. In the same way, one has only to take a Sunday afternoon walk in one of your beautiful forests, where anti-litter signs are written in your language only to come to the conclusion that the picnickers who chose that spot cannot have been French.

And those enamel plates in your train and bistro lavatories requesting the user to leave them in the same state of cleanliness as that in which one found them on entering, have always, I must confess, left me puzzled as to what I ought to do when I have finished. But I understand now: due no doubt to some spiteful trick of fate, I have always followed one of those damned foreigners who cannot read French, and sully your forests and your W.C.s. And how much better I now understand your cry of 'dirty foreigner!'

You see, I have taken the first step: I am beginning to share your xenophobia.

Mind you, there is nothing mean-minded about your xenophobia these days. You are no longer content to quarrel with Monaco or Andorra: you have raised your sights.

Power politics demand that France no longer direct her ready facility for being 'anti' against minorities; now she must antagonize majorities as well. Thus by supporting the blacks in the United States, the citizens of Quebec in Canada and the Vietcong in Indo-China, she automatically becomes anti-American, anti-British, indeed anti-anyone you care to mention. To-morrow she may just as easily become anti-Canadian or anti-Soviet if she can manage it.

So much for power. It is important to note that, at a time when France is doing her best to pluck the old anti-Anglo-Saxon strings, individuals, business firms and advertising have never been more Anglo-Saxonized. This is just one of the paradoxes of a country which is so logical that at a time when it is alienating half the world it can declare that it hasn't a single enemy. Though Frenchmen may demonstrate on behalf of the blacks in Alabama this does not prevent them from remaining racialists after their own fashion at home. Pochet, Taupin and Requillard make no bones about their disgust at pictures showing the measures taken to suppress Negro rights in the United States. They themselves would not have so deprived those poor coloured people—within certain limits, of course: their daughters, for example. It is rather curious how, to one and all of them, the colour problem seems liable to affect the fate of their offspring and threaten their daughters.

"Oh, I'm not saying," they say, "that I'd be pleased if my daughter came to me tomorrow and said she intended to marry a black. I'm not a racialist, but all the same there are limits!"

Tramps' limits, limits of breeding, which dagoes, Negroes and gypsies are requested not to cross.

Yesterday I was in one of your charming bistros in the Grenelle district, along with a few North Africans and a lot of Frenchmen. One of the latter, forcing his way along the counter, jogged the arm of a dark-skinned man and spilled his drink. An argument ensued, and rapidly became acrimonious. From "Mind what you're doing, can't you?" it soon reached "Why don't you stay back home where you belong?" Finally the Algerian, having failed to get his drink replaced, said to the Frenchman who had bumped into him, "Oh, b—— off, you bastard!"

"I may be a bastard," came the reply, "but I'm a French bastard!"

I must confess that this form of identification left me flabbergasted. An Englishman would never make a claim like that. And where am I going to get the courage for such presumption?

After all, there are only two possible alternatives.

Either it's all a matter of pure chance and something for which one is in no way responsible, and therefore nothing to be proud of; or one has to admit that there are people astute enough to insist before emerging from the womb: "I want to be white, Catholic and French!"

Well, I take my hat off to you! This is a championship that I can't compete in. All my life I must have lacked some quality essential to being like you.

There's no question about it, the best thing about being French is that one isn't a Foreigner!

III

SUPPOSING EVERYBODY ... OR, THE LAND OF GRUMBLERS

I AM ONLY TOO CONSCIOUS that I still have a devil of a long way to go before I am ready to join your ranks.

We are a country of humour, but you are a country of humours. The former is sometimes difficult to grasp, but the latter are often impossible to follow. I am, moreover, not speaking only of those moments of high fever when M. Taupin is capable of marching in procession up the Champs-Elysées behind the Star of David, shouting "Support Israel! Down with the Arabs!", forgetting that in bygone days his grandfather, an anti-Dreyfus officer, used to shout, "Long live the Army! Down with the Jews!", and unable to foresee that a year later the doings of one Cohn-Bendit will cause him to revert to those same excesses.

It must be admitted that this is just one man's approach—or *démarche,* as you have been saying ever

since you started taking your thoughts for a walk[1] I
shall come back later to these emotional peak periods.
For the moment, however, I would rather try to follow
you at a more moderate pace—that's quite difficult
enough.

I'm sorry to have to raise the matter, but there are
moments when I wonder whether your good-natured
country is not, by and large, rather bad-tempered. In
fact, the whole nation sometimes seems to me to be
on the point of exploding.

And against whom, for heaven's sake? Your front-
iers are no longer threatened by hostile armies; your
soil is no longer occupied by foreign troops, now that
the last Anglo-Saxon units have been firmly asked to
withdraw from the hexagon; even tourists have become rare specimens; and France at last belongs to
the French. So at whom are their rumbles and grum-
bles aimed?

At themselves, obviously.

Lacking a hereditary enemy—which they can ill
do without—the French have discovered one in themselves, and an indomitable one, since there is no way
of kicking it out of France except by fleeing the
country.

Comme c'est drôle!

When the General was not raging against the
Americans or the English, he was raging against the
French. And now that the French have stopped being
at loggerheads with the General, they are at logger-

[1] "Vous faites faire footing a votre pensée." An Anglicism
that does not exist in English, which is why it tends to catch
me on the wrong foot. (The Major's footnote.)

heads with his enemies. The socialists rage against the communists. The communists against the extremists. The extremists and the communists against the capitalist middle classes. The upper middle classes against the leftist intellectuals. The leftist intellectuals against the lower middle classes. The lower middle classes against the upper. And the middle classes as a whole are so much up in arms against the term 'middle class' that for a member of them to call himself one is almost as rare as for a conservative to admit that he tends to the right.

The peasants, raging against the rest of the country, are by no means loath to join in this festival of ill-will, but I must record that in everyday life your countryfolk, less exposed to jostling and bustling, are not as highly charged with electricity as the residents of your City of Light.

"Paris is not France." M. Taupin is always telling me. Well, I only hope he is right.

If, to achieve the *mutation* that the General wants, I could confine my metamorphosis merely to becoming a citizen, it would give me considerable relief, or, as he says, *bien du plaisir*. Because, between ourselves, being a real Parisian involves having a curious mental make-up, and, as you well know, 'curious' includes 'bad-tempered', just as the 'plaisir' apparently includes discontent.

To prove this I need only describe my first day in your capital.

It began, I must admit, in the best way possible for

. .

my *reconversion*[2]—that is to say, extremely badly. Installed in my hotel bedroom, I had scarcely finished
the exiguous national breakfast—so much better for
the figure, with its croissants and coffee, than our blasted porridge, kippers and bacon and eggs—when someone knocked several times on the door. Before I could
say 'come in' the door was flung open and a waiter
appeared, and was thereby treated to the sight of
one of Her Majesty's retired officers as naked as the
General is said to wish me to be if I am to get by the
revisional council of the Common Market. He had, it
seemed, rushed in to fetch the tray, as if it were the
only one the hotel possessed. And herein, lies one of
the great mysteries of your wonderful hotel trade. Is
it really true that dirty foreigners like myself sneak
off with breakfast trays? (As God is my witness, I have
never left your welcoming, if inhospitable, country
with a tray concealed under my coat.) Or is it that
your country, so rich in dishes, suffers from a lament-
able shortage of trays?

Still, I have got used to this, just as I have got used
to stooping to wash my hands in a tiny basin apparently designed for a child rather than a grown-up. One
wonders if the French people, despite their greatness,
are inferior to us in stature? Sport must have had a
remarkable effect on our development. On the other
hand, your baths, too, rarely allow a Major to lie at
full length, and certainly thereby discourage lolling
about and prevent him from growing soft.

That was how things were—and that was how I was

[2] Conversion would suffice—at least, it used to—but I am
trying to keep up with your new jargon. (The Major's note.)

—when, having washed *à la Française*, which is to say, at the double with half a cake of soap, I suddenly remembered that I had some telephone calls to make. The charming switchboard operator got me my three numbers one after the other so quickly that I thanked her at some length, and we fell into conversation.

"You've had breakfast, at least!" she said. "I've been on duty since seven and I haven't had a thing."

Filled with compassion, I rang the bar and asked for this efficiently operating operator to be sent an expresso which, if not very French, could at least be very large.

"A coffee for the telephonist?" A much less agreeable voice, this one. "Suppose everyone began asking us for that?"

And that was my first 'suppose everyone' of the twenty that I must have heard during the course of the day. Not many minutes later a ticket collector in the underground was shutting his barrier in my face, apparently with malicious glee, though the train had scarcely emerged from the tunnel.

"Too late!" he said, with a satisfied grin.

"I'm alone," I pointed out, "and there's no one behind me or on the platform. Surely you could let me through?"

"Ah, supposing everyone asked me that!"

I could have retorted that I was asking him that precisely because at that particular moment there *was* no one else in the station to ask it. But something prevented me (perhaps shame at catching myself begging for an illicit favour). And why should I spoil his enjoyment of one of the few pleasant moments in his dreary day?

An hour later, this time in a bus, I found myself without any small change. When I handed the conductor a ten-franc note he said to me, "Realize what you're doing? Suppose everyone paid with a thousand-franc note?"

I immediately had a vision of this wretched conductor beset by ten million arms holding out thousand-franc notes, and was overcome with regret and sympathy. But behind me someone muttered, "It's the truth, isn't it? .... If these Foreigners can't do the same as everyone else they should stay at home." And I began to realize that I should never do the same as anybody else.

Just because I'm a Foreigner. Plus something about my appearance—perhaps the readiness with which my incisors enjoy the fresh air on my lower lip—that gives Frenchmen the impression that I am secretly amused when in fact I am deadly serious. So I was prepared to put down the ill-temper I inspired to this typically British malformation until, riding in a taxi that afternoon with M. Taupin, I heard the driver say when my friend asked him to wait for three minutes outside a shop: "Supposing everyone asked me to wait for three minutes! I could spend the whole day at it. I know that lark!"

Clearly, Foreigner or not, everyone gets the same treatment. The 'supposing everyone' undoubtedly springs from the French people's famous genius for inference: the taxi-driver whom M. Taupin asked to wait three minutes immediately turned this exception

35

into a hard-and-fast rule. He saw himself waiting three minutes for two hundred clients and naturally his patience was exhausted.

This sense of logic can go even further. A short while ago I accompanied the Taupins to the Chateau de Versailles. As we went in the woman at the door looked disapprovingly at Madame Taupin's shoes. "I hope you aren't wearing stiletto heels. . . . Supposing everyone came in them, that would be a nice kettle of fish!"

Madame Taupin, mark you, was not wearing stiletto heels, but the custodian was so much obsessed by this type of heel that she was secretly disappointed that the visitor was not wearing them. She would not have been at all displeased to have a chance to fly into a rage, just to prove her worth as the appointed guardian of Versailles and France. I do not know what it was that M. Taupin then said to this cerberus, but her face, sullen only a second before, lit up with a broad smile. Fundamentally, the attitude of the French towards the French is roughly the same as towards us:

(1) In my family we have always loathed the British.
(2) Fundamentally, however, we could get on very well together.

It would, perhaps, be simpler if we could get on well together right from the start, but in France anger always comes first and good manners second.

Whatever difficulties may stand in the way of my

venture, I am determined as a worthy son of John Bull not to abandon it. I have made a bet and I do not intend to throw in my hand. Moreover, there are some encouraging signs.

The other day, as I was returning to my hotel, a woman with a suspiciously bulging handbag nonetheless asked me for alms, revealing within the space of a minute that her husband had deserted her, that she received nothing from Social Security and that her daughter was a trollop. In short, unless I gave her five francs (your beggars, like your doctors, always make their request in new francs) she would throw herself in the Seine.

"My good woman," I said to her, "suppose everyone asked for five francs from a retired Major like me. I really don't know how I'd manage!"

The echo of my own words hit me like a boomerang. I was certain that I had heard them somewhere before. Whereupon, on a generous impulse, I handed her, like a good Frenchman, a full fifth of what she had demanded.

One must be fair to Parisians: their daily life puts a heavy strain on their nerves.

Some fifteen years ago I described the miniature war which motorists carry on against pedestrians, pedestrians against motorists, and motorists against each other. But, if I may venture to say so, you have made considerable progress since then. It is a long time since a French driver used merely to enquire, with his index finger levelled at his temple like a screw-driver, whether his neighbour had gone completely nuts. Long past, too, is the time when drivers merely called each other clumsy clots or silly nits. Today, if they do not go any faster, they certainly go much further. It is no longer a question of hurling insults but of exchanging blows. M. Pochet assures me, and I am quite prepared to believe him, that as little as ten years ago no driver would have taken advantage of a traffic jam to get out of his car and deliver a fourpenny one to whoever had obstructed his path (invariably a small man in spectacles, while the assail-ant is tall and hefty). This, it appears, is now current practice. And it doesn't stop there; three or four times a year an angry driver or pedestrian brings the argu-ment to a sudden close by producing a flick-knife or a revolver and liquidating his opponent.

While it does not necessarily lead to such irrepar-able damage, Parisian anger may be said to be revving up like Parisian engines. M. Pochet's ill-humour is ignited by pedestrians who do not know when to cross, and it is sharpened by contact with the increasing number of people who do not know how to drive (especially 'women who have nothing to do'), who have never learned how to park or who, judging by their impatience, have never seen anyone else park-ing. When he himself finds a space at last M. Pochet's anger reaches boiling point at the sight of the traffic warden lying in wait for him. It is only with the greatest reluctance that he will relinquish this hard won parking-place to its next occupant, so infuriated is he that anyone should find—apparently at the first

attempt—a space that he himself has had such difficulty in locating.

In this respect, too, Parisians strike me as extremely
odd. I happen to be a driver myself, and I am just as
keen on my car as M. Pochet is on his. Nevertheless,
when I see a driver waiting for the parking space in
a Paris street that I am about to leave, I am not immediately seized with a desire to vacuum the back
shelf or consult my address-book. I dislike keeping
people waiting and I expect other people to behave
as I do. Is there something about my face or my car
that reminds them all of a sudden that they have forgotten something? Time and time again when I draw
up to take the place of a driver who is about to leave,
my appearance inspires him to rummage for something under the dashboard, adjust his mirror, clean
his windscreen, thumb through his notebook, put on
his gloves and, if he really can find nothing else to do,
leave the space as unwillingly as if he were obliged to
give up his own private property, acquired at great expense, to a squatter from God knows where ... The
French certainly have a highly-developed sense of
property.

But I really shouldn't make fun of the good people
of Paris.

How can they help being under an acute nervous
strain when they are slaves to traffic jams and jostling,
subject to *disque*-checker and Exchequer as their an-
cestors were to the *taille*[3] and the *gabelle*[4], and victims
of air pollution, government interference and a general

[3] The land tax.
[4] The salt tax.

atmosphere of bad temper? What sort of a life is it when you spend it with an eye on the clock, a hand on your wallet and a foot on the brake?

I can well understand that whenever my translator returns to Paris from his country place, he feels as if a huge invisible hand has stuck an electric plug into his back, and shouted, "Get a move on!"

If only he could! But for him, as for everyone else, times have changed. Formerly his car provided a means for him to get to his place of work more rapidly; now he works inside it.

Need I point out that Parisians are the only ones to suffer from these evils? Everyone knows that Londoners, New Yorkers and Romans have no traffic jams, make nil income-tax returns, make a handsome living in idleness and can give themselves up to enjoyment—leaving Parisians to extricate themselves from their difficulties as best they may.

But I have spoken quite enough about the general moods of individuals. The time has come for me to scrutinize the individual moods of your General, whose powerful voice still echoes in my memory, and whose great arms continue, if only in retrospect, to stir up the history of our times.

IV

FRANCE WILL ALWAYS BE FRANCE

FOR THE MEN OF DESTINY who have saved France in general, and for General de Gaulle in particular, I have always felt the keenest admiration, but I am sorry to say I have had a certain amount of trouble[1] persuading my compatriots that his intentions towards them are nothing but good. No doubt, still lacking your relish for good things, they are unable to appreciate them as they should.

Bon Dieu!

When will the world (including the British Isles) finally acknowledge this patently obvious truth? France is the only country in the world which never acts from self-interest, but only in the interests of the universe at large. It may happen—nothing is impossible—that a suggestion put forward by the President

[1] English for 'the greatest imaginable difficulty.' (M. Denainos' note.)

is initially in his nation's interest; but later this merges by great good fortune into the general interest. France helps everyone on earth, after first helping herself. Certain carping critics feel that there is something supernatural about this, but it is a fact; Since the time of Saint Genevieve, France and the miraculous have maintained such a close and staunch relationship that everyone regards them as inseparable. The only people who doubt this are a few of my country's old maids and a host of its hypocrites.

My country, right or wrong, must accept that there are only two alternatives:

Either *a solution appears advantageous to France in which case it will be beneficial for the rest of the world.*

Without France where would our light come from, since that country rightfully carried the torch of civilization, which can scarcely be borne by ten people at once?

Or *a solution is adverse to France's genius and vocation, in which case it is no good to anyone.*

Is 'genius' a word that can be applied only to France? Scepticism about this point is not entirely forbidden, but it is quite remarkable that no English or American politician ever declares that a solution is adverse to the genius and vocation of his country. One wonders whether we even possess such qualities. Probably not; otherwise we should have heard something about them. It seems a pity. To resign ourselves to being countries without either genius or vocation would be *un désastre* if we did not know that France is close at hand, smilling and generous, giving us dispensation by dispensing her own.

Proof that there is nothing supernatural about this lies in the entirely natural way the words 'vocation' and 'genius' spring to the lips of French statesmen. They (the words) automatically come to mind, like the Incomparable Charm of your bistros and the Matchless Elegance of Parisan women. Again, one of the General's last speeches adds fuel to my fire, though it needs little enough: most Heads of States, and our Queen herself, when wishing their subjects a happy New Year, express the hope that they will do honour to their destinies. When General de Gaulle used to do so, it was the New Year which was required to do honour to France. Wonderful! It would be difficult to find a better way of proving that your country maintains an exceptionally privileged relationship with Providence.

At least, that is my deep-seated conviction. And it is for this reason that if the solution which France proposes (and of which God, if He so wishes, can, with her collaboration, dispose) appear to us at first sight a trifle bitter, we should not doubt that the time will come for us to gather the sweetest fruits from them.

When, for instance, the President of the Republic, plainly speaking in the name of reason and common sense, offers the Americans no alternative but to withdraw their troops immediately, even if by so doing he inflicts on them the first kick in the pants in their history, he is of course acting in *their* interests, *bien sur*. He would not have tolerated such an ultimatum from the Americans when France found herself in the same position, but that is neither here nor there. It is part of France's history. Who would dare to question it?

When General de Gaulle, visiting by invitation one of the largest countries in the world, took advantage of the occasion to call on one of its provinces to seek autonomy and followed this up by referring on several occasions to those people styled French Canadians by their constitution, as Canadian French, who could call this an unwarrantable interference in the internal affairs of a Sovereign State? Everyone knows that it is only in Paris that Quebec is given her due. The General was only speaking in the interests of the American Continent as a whole; once this new seed of discord was sown, Canada could not fail to become stronger and more united.

Enfin—mais ce n'est pas le moindre,[2] I come to ourselves. . . . When the General insisted that England must be reformed from top to bottom if she wished to be worthy of admission to the Common Market (what a shocking picture! . . . I thought for a moment he had been referring to our minis and our loose ways) one has to be dull-witted and narrow-minded, and in a world surrounded by water (as are, alas, my damned fellow countrymen) not to realize that we are not even half way there.[3]

---

[2] Last, but not least.

[3] It was Bernard Frizell, an American writer working for the National Broadcasting Company, who once explained to me: "It's very easy to meet a Frenchman half way: you walk ninety metres—and he readily agrees to cover the other ten." (The Major's note.)

France Will Always be France

Some Englishmen, forgetting their innate belief in the salutary effects of corporal punishment, have claimed to be insulted when a General to whom we readily lent a mike during our darkest hour, left us cooling our heels at the gates of the continent we helped to save and 'procrastinate'[4] our entry for ever. How can people who are accustomed to bullying and the cane fail to see that, like punishment administered to a refractory child, it is all for their own good? Does not everyone in my kindly country declare that a good hiding never did anyone any harm? When they chastise us, the French are merely proving that they love us. The General emphazised this when he said to Sir Patrick Reilly, our Ambassador in Paris: "You'll see, the English will appreciate all I've done for them one day, and they'll thank me for it."

That is not only the language of a true friend and a man of sound sense, but also that of an inflexibly just tutor. A good family man who loved his children would speak in exactly the same way. I should add that those qualities are in this case so far-reaching that that family man takes care not only of his own fifty million insufferable urchins but of other people's as well. Fabulous!

In short a Paterfamilias on a planetary scale, the General exercised an international paternalism. Little by little he set the tone for his closest associates until, by a kind of mimesis such as is often found in great

[4] 'Procrastinate', which is to say 'continually to put off till the next day', expresses exactly what is meant, but you have given up using it, no doubt because you have set it aside for our future use.

dynasties, they came to reflect as best they could from their rung of the ladder their boss's alternately good-natured and admonitory manner. What must England do? Nothing could be simpler: the way is obvious. . . . And the U.S.A.? All that is asked of them is that they do whatever they do not want to do—because, quite simply, *it is for their own good*. And France? Paraphrasing Victor Hugo (according to whom 'when Paris sneezes, the whole world catches cold') the General wants nothing but her prosperity, because "unless France is happy, there can be no happiness".

Though our flu is extremely virulent, we have never succeeded in giving the whole world migraine when London has a headache. No doubt our radiation is not strong enough. Besides, no country but France would declare so calmly—or at least without arousing any misgivings—that the stronger it becomes, the happier the world will be. Switzerland, Sweden, perhaps Monaco; but who would take them seriously if Great Britain, the United States or Germany talked in that way?

We must agree, then: only France can do it—because she is France, and because France is a Woman. Courageous and noble, innocent and chaste, she is incapable of provoking the slightest mistrust. Coveted, lusted after and lain in wait for by seducers of the lowest order who would not hestitate to rape her on the road to Market, she advances serenely down a highway bristling with ambushes and bordered by precipices. What does that matter? It is paved with good intentions. Of course, there are other nations of the same kind—of the feminine gender, I mean—England

and Germany, for instance.[5] But one cannot compare tough Britannia or the German valkyrie with the fragile femininity of France. I should not talk about fragility though: thanks to her hexagonal coffers, France possesses an iron constitution (and has emerged reinvigorated from the abyss). Even her flu reflects the country's nature: gentle and moderate. The only serious flus to have ravaged France have always been foreign invaders (Spanish, Asian, etc.).

It is understandable that such a generous country, which acts in her own interests only to further the interests of others, and which has never set foot on foreign soil except by accident or to promote the welfare of lesser peoples to whom it brought the (sometimes a little too bright) light of its torch, a country which enjoys a three-star *pointe de vue* from the summit of Europe, will always be exposed to the forces of evil, to a worldwide conspiracy and to the morbid envy of unhealthy nations whose contamination extends even to the weather. To judge from French weather forecasts, bad weather always comes from abroad (suggesting that if there were no such place as abroad, the sun would always be shining over France): depressions from Ireland, anticyclones from the Azores, cold air currents from the Shetlands, wet spells from Scotland, heat waves from the United States and cold waves from Scandinavia or Russia—never is the smallest particle of bad weather a native of France. Always that damned Abroad. No wonder France feels

[5]Only in French, of course; a language that uncompromisingly attributes genders to the names of countries is perceptive indeed.

cold towards it (though the cold is usually caught by us).

That is why the General must be believed—as if one would disbelieve someone who dealt exclusively in elementary truths. What used to amaze me most, perhaps, about the General's style was the lucidity with which he presents his case. If an English or American politician took it into his head to declare in a major speech that England should be English (or America American), everyone would roar with laughter. Only one man could thrust his way through such open doors without provoking hilarity, and that was your General. When, for instance, he proclaimed that Europe should be European, not only was this bold doctrine accepted without demur at the time, within a few weeks the most serious leader-writers were repeating it. This man's simplest axioms acquired a mysterious power, so that when—things being as they are—he graciously assured us that we were a great people, we all felt a good deal better.

You were fortunate in possessing not only the greatest living statesman but also the youngest.

If de Gaulle had been twenty, all the shortcomings of youth would have been found in him: impudence, impetuosity, a tendency to self-contradiction, ingratitude towards old Uncle John Bull, an irresistible propensity for solving other people's problems whether his advice was sought or not, a self-indulgent love of creating disorder by the discovery of problems previously undreamed of, the petulance of a spoilt child, a desire to show off or, as you say, *epater la galerie*—

are not these the distinguishing characteristics of the very young?

What other statesman, at the start of a press conference in his palace, under the floodlights, T.V. cameras and microphones, would in referring to Great Britain, have recalled the advantages that a naked woman enjoys—knowing that he himself would be decently protected by the dispensation that is accorded to minors?

Take another example of his youthful impetuosity —Quebec. A casual observer might have thought, when he roared "Long live free Quebec!" in Montreal that your Head of State, carried away by the warmth of his welcome, had allowed his words to outrun his thoughts, that this was a blunder or a slip of the tongue.

There are unquestionably bounds which should not be exceeded when one is the guest of a foreign country —bounds of propriety. If, for instance, M. Taupin had heard that his sixteen-year-old son, spending the summer with an English family in Northern Ireland, had cried out at the end of his first dinner there: "Long live free Northern Ireland!" . . . he would immediately have taken a pen or the first plane to rebuke the young scoundrel, remind him of his manners and apologize in the name of France for his tactlessness. For only a painfully badly brought-up youngster (and God knows his father has taken enough pains) could drop such a brick.

But we are not concerned with M. Taupin's son. Your grand young man cannot be compared to someone so unimportant.

49

Far from apologizing, as any of our old-fashioned gentlemen, still obedient to their papas' code of politeness, would undoubtedly have done, he repeated the offence at the first available opportunity; or, rather, he went still further in another speech when he bluntly offered his best wishes to the *French nation of Canada*.

Quite incredible!

I am well aware that, from the humblest to the greatest, men are but backward children. They prove it almost daily. What I have said about the General might be said of others. For instance. . . .

If your fifteen-year-old son—he is very bright for his age, of course—had an idea for a revolutionary improvement in teaching methods, and came home one day in triumph to announce that his proposals had been approved by 99.989 per cent throughout the classrooms of Paris, would you believe him? You most certainly would not. If it were my own son, I should first wonder just how hard I ought to box his ears. After all, you and I are not open-mouthed simpletons. But that is what President Nasser made his people swallow, and perhaps the rest of the world, too, since all the newspapers announced that he had been confirmed in office by 99.989 per cent of the Egyptian electorate. I wonder why he did not settle straight away for a round 100 per cent. He must have taken into account the 0.011 per cent too paralysed to mark the voting papers.

Now take the case of a young man, fresh out of school or college, sent to Vietnam in the middle of the fighting to solve the military equation: *if the*

United States up till now have been unable to beat the Vietcong with 500,000 men, 3,000 bombers and fighters and 5,000 helicopters, and are up against forces three times as numerous but 70 per cent inferior in technical resources, what do they need to achieve victory?

Suppose the young man comes back after two years' careful study of the situation and confidently announces:

"To win the war, the U.S.A. will require exactly 206,000 more men."

Not 207 or 205, but exactly 206,000. Would you not begin to suspect that this jackanapes had fallen on his head and was pulling our legs? Nevertheless this figure of 206,000 was prepared, weighed and announced in all seriousness by General-Proconsul Westmoreland, a short time before he was honourably relieved of his command with all the respect due to his rank. And this figure, which would be highly comic if it were not so tragically ludicrous, was given a three-column spread simultaneously by every newspaper on this planet.

I have quoted these two examples to show that the juvenile failings of your General are not unique. All mankind ever does is to change its toys: it swaps scooters for de luxe fluid-drive saloons, dolls and teddy bears for gigolos and dolly girls, kites for jets, school prizes for academicians' hats, and diplomatic examination papers for a noble page in history when the time comes for a dignified exit.

Things are the same, alas, at the Elysée as at the

White House: in Moscow, Lisbon or Peking, all of us, great and small will die children (though of course *enfants de la Patrie*).

Meanwhile we will continue to wait for the day—and it will come—when the whole world is our country.

V

MARRIAGEABLE FRANCE

 WHEN I LAST RETURNED to France and her *poules*[1] I found the France of Mont-de-Marsan and Beziers, of Bégles and Narbonne, of Toulouse and Carcassonne and all those *poules* which, dressed in black and white, cruise the Sunday television sports programmes, making perfectly decorous offers of entertainment—offers which on the evening of my arrival, I found myself accepting.

Too tired to go out, I was reduced, in fact, to rediscovering France, also reduced, in this case to the size of her small screen. If I had gone out, would I have been able to find your very pretty *poulettes* again? Apparently they have become very scarce and, if they are real dears, very dear. So it was in a much more sporting, you might say healthy, guise that France reappeared to me; heroic France, whose ever-

[1] 'Poule' can mean both 'football-league' and 'tart'.

courageous XV can only lose through some appalling misunderstanding, an inexorable stroke of fate or the unforgivable mistake of a neutral referee—Swiss, Dutch, Belgian or English—who is dishonest, malicious and quite capable of awarding an unjustifiable penalty against you out of pure bloody-mindedness, and who is justly reprimanded by your newspapers next morning. One headline, amongst many others, presents the matter in its true light:

> Incredible bad luck and an extraordinary
> decision by the Englishman, Mr. Lamb
> YES, THE FRENCH XV BEATEN
> (6–3) BY SCOTLAND
> SHOULD BE CONGRATULATED

Fortunately France hero-worships her unlucky heroes, so that in your history books the perpetual second comes into first place. The memorable saying, 'France has lost a battle, but she has not lost the war', becomes in peacetime, 'France has been beaten, but it is not a defeat'.

Once again I was confronted with that indomitable France for whom Sedan is now nothing more than a crack football XI which from time to time comes up against Strasbourg, and Joffre a wing three-quarter,[2] 'whose lightning acceleration' according to one newspaper 'broke the trap set by the Rumanians' (when behind the Iron Curtain, France is always up against crafty Foreigners full of ruse if not russified;

---

[2] Confirmed by the Sports Edition. (Editor's note.)

54

when front of it, against hypocritical and cunning Anglo-Saxons).

Reading the *Figaro* and other newspapers, I found a glorious France, tough in the scrums and so extraordinarily mixed up that a visitor like me has difficulty in getting his bearings when suddenly told that Rouen is away to Nîmes, Angoulême to Bordeaux, and Nantes to Sochtaux, and that, at Toulouse, Vichybasket had had to 'concede its place' to Le Mans.

All things considered it was natural that I should find France at a crossroads, for she has always lived at one, closely watched by Foreigners impatient to see her stumble and drop the torch that lights up the whole world. This time a big, bad, hungry wolf— and a female into the bargain—the Industrial Society has, if certain speakers are to be believed, made several dates with France merely in order to break them. Apparently, though you are a big girl now you are afraid—the things people say!—of bumping into this great electronic camel of an Over-Developed Society, and you are fully prepared to betray her even before the wedding.

In this connection, may I say what a great pleasure it is to come back to your zoological vocabulary. My countrymen love horses, cats and dogs more than you—so much so that when promoting a new Daimler there is nothing to beat a dapple-grey pony bowing its head to a cover-girl at the wheel—but only in the language of Buffon can one express oneself about the New Society in such animal terms.)

And as for the impending marriage with that damned Society,—excuse me if I change horses in mid-stream but, with such a snake in the grass, one must put up the hare—I will tell you what I think: France's happiness is no more dependant on nuclear reactors than on pie-in-the-sky.

Those barbaric Anglo-Saxon Americans want to contaminate you with their so-called technical progress. I should like to know just how early-warning systems, protonic synchrotrons and catalytic filtering machines will improve your cosy little lives (dammit, I nearly said 'way of life').

I can only beg you with all my military strength (somewhat rusty, perhaps, but not yet green with age) not to say to those prospective destroyers what your General Cambronne, losing his men but not his power of speech, called out to one of our Generals at Waterloo.[3] Just go on quietly living your sublime lives with no other programming than the occasional nice little nip from that hidden bottle of yours.

Incidentally one has to get up early in the morning to be able to produce as many things from hidden stores as you do—I write as a *rosbif* and one who has never shrunk from rising with the dawn to get a breath of fresh air. But only yesterday, who produced a bottle of Pouilly-Fumé for me from nowhere? The comely Mère Touillard. Can you tell me where else that could happen? In Missouri, Surrey, the Ukraine? If you'll forgive me. Please excuse the expression—nuts!

The Industrial Society has an attractive image, but

[3] "Pray, fire first!"

yours will always be better. For Heaven's sake keep it as it is for as long as you can, and do not let yourselves be corrupted by the fiendish enticements of the atomic daemons. They may be able to invent super-computers with supraconductible coils, neutron detectors and plutonigenic reactors, but there will never be electronic vintages, magnetic craftsmanship or particulate syntax. Hold fast to the upward slope, you sprightly millegenarian;[4] you have risen for many centuries without a lift, and thanks to M. Eiffel's ingenuity you have risen higher than anyone else in the world.[5]

Though, as the Church's elder daughter, it is natural for you to obey orders, you were not born to obey those damned computers.

It is not that I am an enemy of progress *proprement dit*, as you so oddly put it (though the phrase[6] is especially appropriate here, since I am about to address myself to the subject of your bathrooms). All I want of you, and in particular of Denainos, by way of progress at the moment, is that the flat belonging to his Ducal landlord which Denainos is about to sublet to me, should contain a bath in which I can stretch full length. He, himself, small though he is, cannot even stretch to his full shortness in the one which he has just installed. He did in all fairness point this out

[4] I do not know how the Major arrives at this figure, but he must set France's origin, anyway under that name, no further back than the Capetians. (Translator's note.)

[5] At least until those damned Yankees put up the Empire State Building. (The Major's heart-broken note.)

[6] *Proprement* means both 'properly' and 'cleanly'.

to the plumbers; however they simply said "You should have warned us. You ought to have ordered the Belgian 'Apollo' or the Swiss 'Tell 69': both these models are longer."

Those dirty Foreigners are always up to something! And in your bathroom, of all places! As if you had not made it clear ages ago that you could get along very well without them! At the time of the last survey in 1948, if I am not mistaken and if a number of estate agents in the heart of Paris can be believed, 75 per cent of the flats in your Capital did not possess a bath of any kind, and in 55 per cent of them the tenants had but a single communal privy per floor. All the same, I am reluctant to believe those well-informed and apparently well-washed experts who say that these modest percentages have not improved. Suppose they have not? Would this be a good enough reason for me to criticize and denigrate ('systematically', according to a small number of anonymous letters, always in the same writing, which my translator has received, together with many kinder ones) France and the French?

France has her reasons of which soap knows nothing. It is all very well to throw bouquets at those baths-for-two where American couples meet morning and evening to make conversation (though I never knew Americans to have any conversation), steeped in hot water; and to hymn the praises of interplanetary rockets, and air-conditioning; but, believe me, nothing can touch France with her woollen stockings, her washing-machines and her dark bistro cabins with electric door-latches. Clearly this country, surfeited with greatness, *deliberately* manufactures the most minute wash-basins, the most ejaculatory lavatory-flushes and the smallest pipi-rooms.

As for that electronic milch-cow, that mechanical Trojan horse, that great automatic monster of an Industrial and Functional Society—no gentle lamb, for she has her eye on your millions—don't marry her unless (forgive me for being frank) you want to be brutally deceived; for the day will come when you say of her, as you do of those women who immediately become 'tarts' as soon as they have made you unfaithful to your wives, "She's ruined my life!"

Of course the elder daughter of the Church could not possibly be anything but the younger daughter of progress.

But in this respect the possible is not your concern. In this crazy, recycled, ionized universe you specialize in the impossible: living your good French lives, many of you without telephones, and perhaps the happier for not having them; and, if you do get one, frequently failing to get the right number. This is another field in which you are unequalled: not only do you manage to exist—and exist better than other people—with fewer telephones per head than the Swedes and Germans, but you undoubtedly are the only nation whose telephones are hypersensitive to rain.

Hypersensitive and, at the same time, astute. Newspaper articles speak disparagingly of your telephone system, and continually harp on the fact that you have fewer instruments per head than the Danes or the

Swiss. But for one thing, any one of your heads is worth ten of theirs. And secondly, if your telephone is not fully automated, it is certainly magical. If you want proof, only the other day when visiting my friend and translator's small house in Saint-Sauveur-sur-Ecole—where the recently installed automatic telephone is not always wholly reliable—I dialled a Fontainebleau number and got a Rambouillet one. And not just any old number: a voice told me, "You've got the wrong number. This is Yvelines Engineers."

But it was not as wrong a number as all that, as you will see, or, rather hear. Denainos had a friend in Yvelines who could not get his line repaired and whose child was seriously ill; so he took the opportunity to explain the position. Believe it or not, his friend's line was repaired within the hour.

Well, there you are. Name another country where, by dialling 422-20-22, you get 483-04-13,[7] I will stand you a Scotch from my own hidden store. Because, when you come to think of it, helping a sick child in Rambouillet by calling a lawyer in Fontainebleau takes quite a bit of doing. And you are the only people capable of doing it. *Messieurs-dames les Français*, I take off my hat to you!

[7] The actual numbers respectively of a lawyer in Fontainebleau and the telephone engineers in Rambouillet. (Confirmatory note by the translator.)

VI

HOW CAN ONE BE TIBETAN?

 SOME OF YOU may have been surprised—if the French can still be surprised by anything—that on my return after so long an absence I should talk about nothing but rugby football, bathtubs and telephones.[1] I do apologize—I am so sorry. Having arrived on a Sunday, I was merely taking things in chronological order. And I hope you will also excuse me (oh, the English passion for hypocritically begging pardon or pardoning others for not having begged pardon) for having merely described, when this welcome reunion took place, the France of rugger and soccer, that broken up geographical jigsaw-puzzle in which Avignon staggers Dax and Ajaccio brings down Nimes.

Talking of jigsaw puzzles, I should have done better

[1] In Chapter V.

to describe how, on board the superjet which brought me from the banks of the Indus back to those of the Seine, I looked down from the skies on my beloved France (if I may briefly use this lofty possessive) with her patchwork, her mosaic, her galaxy of squared-off fields where green mingles with ochre and yellow, the France of real cultivation, industrious, thrifty and lavish, with not an acre wasted, the splendid parks and forests of emerald and gold—incomparable France as she alone can be. Should I start all over again and talk about more serious matters? Very well, here goes. I did not just find France unlucky at rugger through bad refereeing, nor an equine France humiliated by a colt and a mare from Her Majesty's realm, which carried off 160 million good old francs from under her nose and turned the Prix de l'Arc de Triomphe[2] into a wake; nor the fact that that was followed almost immediately afterwards by the victory of another British thoroughbred in the Prix de Verdun. I also found, alongside Eternal France, an entirely new France, endowed with a young, dynam., compet., gd. refs. Gaullist govt.—in short, one deserving to find the best job among those small advertisements that are so dear to the *Figaro* and contribute so substantially to its fortunes. A France in full expansion, functional, competitive and standing up to progress with the most modern postal inventions: a two-speed post with electronically-controlled auto-

[2] Need I to mention that your best thoroughbreds, badly placed at the turn, 'could not make the running'? Of course not.

matic sorters. After that, do not tell me that France
has not taken the New Society wholeheartedly to her
bosom. Here again, as in other fields, you have been
able to emancipate yourselves ahead of everyone else,
and point the way to the rest of the world by a frank
revolution.

Since the French miracle—or at least one of them
for there are hundreds—is her ability always to con-
jugate the past in the present, I came back to a completely up-to-date France celebrating the virtues of
our toughest enemy and reliving Napoleonic times in
the most natural way in the world. I was going to say
'in the oddest way', for it seems very curious to a
Foreigner that a nation which is democratic in practice, if not in spirit, should be re-reading with religious
fervour the epic of the little corporal, and that a President of the Republic should fly to Ajaccio to celebrate
the virtues of an Emperor who, although indubitably
glorious, was also somewhat bloodthirsty around the
edges.

Leaving England aside, let me tell you that the
name of Napoleon still spreads terror in Saragossa
and Marengo,[3] where his soldiers, doubtless exceeding
their instructions, managed without benefit of the

---

[3] Which has become for you not only the name of a victory
but a way of cooking chicken and veal according to the recipe
employed by Bonaparte's cook on the eve of the battle : cut
up, seize over a hot fire and finish by cooking in oil with mush-
rooms and truffles.

latest electrical innovations to commit some pretty unsavoury atrocities.[4]

If it is never too late to make amends, however poorly, I should like at this stage to pay homage to that man of whom I have spoken so ill and whom the English have so often underestimated (to the point of total devaluation), while at the same time regretting from the bottom of their hearts—and sometimes on the surface of my beloved *Times*—that they have no one of his calibre to lead them.

Let me now say that what was saddest about the twilight of that greatness was its smallness. Yet it lacked neither fair play nor nobility. "Say yes or no. I shall remain or leave for ever."

I hope that I shall be believed, though I'm sure I shan't be : I was really sorry to see so great an actor muff his exit. But do you yourselves remember it? You are said to have short memories, and I must confess, that Prague, which shook you to the core, certainly seems to have been forgotten both by your most hardened protesters and by the extreme-left middle classes, living comfortably in their flats on the same bank as their politics, who bitterly blaming America for its intervention in Vietnam and swallowing the

[4] Though not in the least an admirer of Napoleon, the translator was concerned to recall the Major to a sense of proportion and recollection of the 'Civil Code'. Napoleon, a fickle husband, nonetheless left behind him a Code which the French, good and bad husbands alike, have to obey willy-nilly.

occupation overnight of Tibet by Mao's armies without giving a damn.

Besides, who on earth would want to be born a Tibetan? It requires a twisted mentality (as twisted as mine, which has a fondness for the Himalayas), suddenly and stupidly to feel that one's heart has become Tibetan and turn one's thoughts towards Tibet, where women and children are dying and rotting; a good-natured people, whose only crime lies in not having Mao and his golden rule under their skin.

Oh, Tibet, you are really forgotten! You should apologize for being so small and thank Heaven that you have been invaded, since it is all for the good of Peking and the Parisian maoists.

If Mao's Chinese, for whom your militant leftists have such an affection, compel monks and nuns, under a vow of celibacy, to marry, what does it matter? What does it matter if the sacred manuscripts of Lhasa have been torn up, xylographs burnt and temples looted? What does it matter if the frontier separating Tibet from India is mined and the 'mad' supporters of independence tortured, those who have not already set fire to themselves? What does it matter if the Tibetans are forced to give up their own language and learn Chinese? Will people believe it, any more than they will believe the recent broadcasts[5] from Radio Tashkent (U.S.S.R.), which announced on April 4th, 1967: "Hundreds of Tibetans have been killed or driven to suicide after torture, while thousands of others have fled in peril of their lives"?

[5] All the facts were set out at length by Sonam Wangdi in the *Tibetan Review*, published in Darjeeling, Bengal.

Certainly not: for it is well known that the Russians do not 'hold with' the Chinese, that the whole thing is propaganda and that law and order reigns in Tibet, happily ensured by Mao's officers and soldiers, who according to the letter of the law (page 185) of the little red book, ('published in Peking and printed in French by the Popular Republic of China') 'must destroy all their enemies resolutely, radically, integrally, totally' (and, of course, with the greatest sincerity).

Every army in the world—German, English, American or, my goodness, I nearly said French—left to itself and especially to the people whom it has come affectionately to occupy, commits acts of cruelty. But we know that the worst of military men, whether they come from Prussia, Paris or Peking, have some good in them. So one must be chary of generalizing and always remember that grandmothers, aunts and cousins bent over the cradles of Attila and Hitler and exclaimed "What a sweet little baby!"

Besides, Tibet is so far away.... The Tibetan God is certainly not ours. Tibet—Hitler—I don't know ... it is time to close this parenthesis: it is letting in a nasty draught.

Tibet, in any case, is not the relevant question. When I asked M. Taupin yesterday to enlighten me and explain exactly why the General had left, he dried up lamentably. What was the Referendum about, I asked: was it for the Languedoc or for the Franche-Comté? A re-cycling of the Senate or a redistribution of everything? Taupin admitted that he had not the vaguest idea, explaining only, zoological as ever, that he had more important fish to fry and younger hares to raise.

FRANCE UNDER FRENCH OCCUPATION

 I HAVE OFTEN secretly thought France's misfortunes sprang from the fact that she was inhabited by fifty million Frenchmen. As de Gaulle wrote in his *War Memoirs*: *"In no event will volunteers bear arms against France. This does not mean that they are forbidden to fight against Frenchmen."*

So my great discovery wasn't so new after all, and I still had much to do before I could adapt myself to the constantly changing totality of your glorious country; recent events, however, have made a powerful contribution towards the forcible completion of my education (the force being of the revolutionary variety). For though I fancied that I had a wide knowledge of France, I still had a devil of a lot to learn about those damned Frenchmen. The fact is that the one does not always give a very accurate impression of the other.

The most notable thing that I learned from the events of 1968 was that France is undoubtedly the only nation in the world which, in the absence of any foreign invader, can manage to live as if she were in a state of occupation.

Anyone who has not seen France so effectively occupied by herself that the Head of State was compelled to decamp to manoeuvres in Germany, and M. Pochet was reduced to knocking on the door of a black-market garage-proprietor in the middle of the night to get a can of petrol, hasn't seen anything and has missed an experience. I am truly grateful to Providence and the occupation forces for providing me with it, and thus playing a part in my reconversion.

And what a show it was! The burning question was, of course, who should occupy whom? The workers occupied the offices of the employers; the employers, locked in, occupied their time as best they could; in due course the students occupied the Sorbonne; the Odeon became the theatre of the occupation; those who had no occupation occupied themselves by going to see what the occupants looked like; and I know of one enterprising executive who, abandoning his normal duties as manager of an agency in order to occupy his firm's head office, discovered on his return to his branch office that it had been occupied by a co-operative more leftish than his own. Is that *bad luck* or *well played*? 'I shall not stick my neck out' (as we English elastically put it) by expressing an opinion.

But, as a bona fide Britisher—if you will pardon the juxtaposition—anxious to conform to European, and therefore French customs, for the well-being of the Common Market, I shall try to understand and to achieve your highly-developed talent for paradox, a domain in which, if you are not kings—since the word is no longer in circulation in your country—you are at least constitutional monarchs. It will be no easy task.

I never dreamed that, only twenty-five years after a war which saw your gallant nation groaning under the pack-boot, a populace that had been humiliated by the mere word 'occupation' would stick the most hated noun in its history on the facades of its factories, stations, universities and post offices.

I could certainly never have imagined that that country, whose communists are as sensitive about their *tricolore* as its conservatives, would see its working-classes rise up with one accord against tyranny and strike in the shade of the red flag of a foreign power which—at home—categorically denies the right to strike. It should also be noted that this scarlet emblem was frequently accompanied by the black standard of anarchy. Unconsciously Stendhalian, rebellious France plays with the red and the black, and does so with the utmost calm.

And, finally, though I was aware of France's flexibility, since she has oscillated between revolution and dictatorship for 179 years, how could I have foreseen that M. Taupin, having suddenly become enough of a revolutionary to kiss his children tenderly as they went off to man the barricades, would transform himself a fortnight later into a fierce supporter of law and order?

I suppose this shows once again that I still have a lot to learn before I can join your ranks. "Try, try and try again!", as our illustrious Churchill used to say. I did try, with the result that, caught up in some demonstration or other, bristling with placards ('To act is to strike', 'Anarchy is order' and so forth) I found myself singing the Marseillaise to the tune of the *International*. No doubt it was foolish of me; but I hope it indicates that I am making some progress in acquiring your paradoxicality. At least I am contrary enough to notice that of all the crazy expenditure incurred by the French that year, the most spendthrift item cost them nothing: it was the prodigious output of verbal energy. On the other hand, if it is true that time is money, what extravagance! Never before have I attended at such a feast of words.

My friends the Pochets, like Colonel Turlot, have assured me more than once in this connection that the country had gone out of its mind (though of course that did not include themselves). But I think they must have been mistaken, or turned up late for the civil war: it seemed to me that minds had never been so supercharged, and that reasoned argument had never used so much constructive dialogue to explain away so many devastating follies.[1]

---

[1] Undoubtedly there were some minor errors of judgment. I am prepared to believe—as my translator does—that the Hitlerian domination and the excesses of two colonial wars have

The students were the first examples of this, selling their revolutionary doctrine on television, and clumsily giving birth to those famous Siamese twin sisters of— technocratic vocabulary, Structure and Change; and the verbal delirium soon infected trade unionists, teachers, politicians and engineers. The only people who seemed immune from this fever were the elderly and the children—and only children in their infancy, for one saw schoolchildren suffering severe attacks of the disease and stammering out their first moral stands as if they had been weaned on a contextual feeding-bottle.

As M. Taupin said to me one day, astonished by the vocabulary of his own children, "They must stuff these cherubs' heads full of nonsense as soon as they leave kindergarten!"

The whole country had become one vast theatre, in which Frenchmen played to a French audience.

---

infected some people with sado-masochistic germs which will not easily be eradicated. Nevertheless, one would need to have a very short memory to bracket the C.R.S., who have admittedly a tendency to hand out fourpenny ones with the S.S., who were liberal dispensers of death. Or no memory at all? . . . At a time when there is so much talk of reforms, there may perhaps be a chance to enlighten your impetuous young people still further on the 'lugubrious' (thank you, General!) delights of those totalitarian régimes from which their fathers snatched them, and towards which an unhealthy frame of mind sometimes seems to be impelling them—particularly when their leaders depict universal suffrage as a form of treason. But this is none of my business and I must apologize to the French for this untimely intrusion into France's affairs, for which after all, they cannot always be blamed.

I often wondered—particularly at lunchtime, when employers and managers vied with each other in re-enacting the scenes of which they had been the heroes earlier that morning ("I made no bones about it: I called in my heads of departments and . . .")—whether the French were not living unwittingly on a vast stage.

But now I have no more doubt about the answer: they are indeed a nation of actors, and in time of trouble they turn the whole country into a national stage (and have no hesitation in occupying subsidized theatres to achieve it).

Or are they, rather, fifty million potential barristers, at their best in wrangling and procedural disputes, to whom the courtroom atmosphere is second nature? Any head of a French family, speaking of his son's studies, will automatically say "He is doing *his* law"; whereas his British or American counterpart, laying no claim to such deeds of title, will merely say "He is studying law".

Barristers? Or actors?

The two natural aptitudes overlap each other to such an extent that I can no longer remember whether the theatre for the oratorical feat which I am about to describe was the Law Courts or the Chamber of Deputies. Not that it matters: for this will always remain in my memory as one of the most sparkling illustrations of French character.

Two orators were engaged in a duel without quarter (there is no other kind). The first sat down, having launched a matchless flight of arrows, but his opponent, though apparently defeated, succeeded in reversing the situation with such brilliance that five minutes later his whole audience was roaring with laughter at the expense of the man it had just been clapping.

Whereupon the latter, obtaining the President's leave to break in—so this must in fact have taken place in the Chamber—said from where he was sitting, "I apologize to my colleague for interrupting him. . . . But he is so witty that I wanted to ask him whether he could spare the time tomorrow evening to drop in on us and amuse the children."

After that the audience did not know where they were.

But I am where I was: in the National Assembly, watching the special performance of May '68, which was open to the public, since the jousts of oratory were being televised. 'Jousts' is not so anachronistic here: it would require the style and palette of a Froissart or a Commines to depict this mediaeval tournament with the knights of the government and the warriors of the various parties leaping into the lists from the height of their platforms.

While heralds of every category confronted each other, appealing incessantly to the 'vast majority' of the nation and the 'sovereignty of the people', the good people, watched the spectacle in the arena from on the touchlines and listlessly reckoned up the score before going off to lay in a stock of noodles or petrol. For it is true, as my friend M. Blot has remarked, that the threat of war in Egypt or the imminence of a revolution in his own country is first reflected, as far as the average Frenchman is concerned, in a run on macaroni or sugar. You never know. . . .

But how did the masses themselves not get carried

away by this torrent of words? In troubled times their stage is the street. Circles form in the squares, at the centre of each an *extempore* orator, encouraged by the constantly expanding circumference. At this moment, when the anger of the masses is supposed to be rumbling, these cross-grained masses have in fact never been kindlier. No one is in agreement, but everyone understands each other. Though I usually meet only sullen faces and passers-by disinclined to help me when I am lost, I have never met so many pleasant people as at that time, all prepared to accompany me for a short distance to put me on my way, and to tell me, as if I were John Bull himself, "we do like you really".

As I saw everyone doing his routine and waiting for the audience to react, I sometimes wondered whether the whole of France was not playing at 'Lets pretend. . . ! The students manned the barricades as if to restore the Commune. The opposition solemnly declared that it was ready to assume its responsibilities, as if office were there for the taking. The trade union leaders ordered the workers to rise up against the tyranny of the powers-that-be, as if royalty were restored to the throne and on the brink of reviving prerogatives. And all the Deputies declared that the country was in danger, as if the Germans were at the gates of Paris.

It goes without saying that a foreigner has no business pretending that France is nothing but a troupe of actors playing fifty million parts and then trying to prove it. I'd much rather you said it for me! But as a matter of fact, you *have* said it and still do, and that confuses me no end. For when, on his return from a folklorique tour of Rumania, your top star, that atomic Druid at bay in the Celtic forest, appeared on the screen to conjure a whole people to adopt him once again and write him a final blank cheque, what was the comment at the end of his seven-minutes performance? "He was bad . . . very bad. . . ."

In the National Assembly the tones of some of the speakers rose during those uneasy times to a grandiloquence more appropriate to tragedy; and was it a damned foreigner who brought them back to earth by crying out, "Gentleman, please! We aren't here to play Homeric heroes!"? On the contrary, it was a perfectly genuine Frenchman, the President of the National Assembly himself.

But the show went on, farcical or serious as the case might be, until the day when it finished as it should: with a dramatic climax. The leading man in the piece, having made what some people believed to be his final exit, suddenly came on-stage again after giving everyone a fright and in four minutes on television wiped out the memory of his clumsy earlier performance and quite retrieved his audience.

Soon order was restored. In France order is both an ideal and a last resort, and so it always ends up by resembling a punishment.

I sometimes wonder whether you are as democratic as you claim to be.

We have a monarchy and practise socialism. You have a republic, but President de Gaulle had one of his speeches prefaced by music from the time of Louis

XIV, and when insurgents invade the streets, they do so to a tune which, when accompanied by clenched fists, does not promise well for individual liberties.

In both cases, I must admit, the music is sung in the name of the people, even if the song is not all that they think it is.

It really is extraordinary what one can appeal to the people for. And when one does not appeal to them, one 'answers for them', 'assumes on their behalf' or simply guarantees their consent. Their cockade belongs to no one, and therefore to everyone, but it does not belong to you. For, though all the citizens together may form a people, the people is not made up only of citizens. (This is only regarded as a vicious circle by those who are excluded from it: how else could one identify the enemies of the people?)

Can it be that the countries in which the people are really powerful are those in which they are not being constantly reassured of their sovereignty?

Imagine the void in which princes would find themselves if the people had no more enemies? From Peking to Paris, by way of Moscow, what confusion would reign! What on earth would princes do if they could no longer declare that the people were in danger, and appeal to their convictions, always *deep*, to their instincts, always *keenly on the alert*, and to their good sense, always *innate*? How insipid life would seem to the princes—trade-union leaders, generals and bikbachis—if they were no longer allowed to announce from time to time that the enemies of the people must be crushed in order to satisfy their invariably *legitimate* claims, their always *essential* needs, and their aims, whose loftiness is never less than the depth of the aforementioned convictions.

Even if it were to occur to a prince to say to his friends (in confidence of course), that the people are vain, weak, vile and like cattle, those cattle are worth their weight in gold in moments of crisis; as sacred in France as the other kind of cows in India. Though there may be something bovine in the people's make-up, the prince himself will hurry to remind us that it is from them that he derives his authority. From one end of the world to the other, east and west, for the staunch third-year maoist as much as for the trade-union leader of Croat origins or the Gaullist sapper, there is only one anonymous king: the people. He can be Spanish, Chinese, Russian, French; muzzle his press, brainwash him every morning in the fields and pass him through the Marxist-Leninist spin-dryer, deny him the right to strike, compel him to undergo three years' military service instead of one for being a despicable conscientious objector—he is still king. Can he doubt it, when his princes assure him that the only desire in their minds is to serve him and ensure his well-being? Nothing can be done except it is in his name. If force is needed to achieve an end, extra pressure is brought to bear on him only with the idea of serving him better. His welfare is the goal and he is himself the often unwitting means of securing it. He is responsible for peace, war and whatever comes in between. He is a monarch who can put his hand to anything, a king-of-all-work, a sovereign who polishes and when worked to the bone, will shine, a highness always ready to lend a hand stirring the pudding, whether it is full of tyrants or sixpences.

From the hard-working womb of this gigantic entity pour idle millionaires and quibbling intellectuals, adventurers and opportunists, the minor nobility and the upper classes; in short, all those who are not 'workers', and therefore do nothing—and everyone, middle-classes, aristocrats, politicians and lobbyists, swears to defend it against the adventurers, opportunists, etc. (see above). Are the liberties of the people threatened? *They* shall not pass! Do they jeer at it? Its innate common sense will put a stop to them. Do they want to silence it? It won't hold its tongue: mute, it can still howl its condemnation. A colossal, seething stew, its anger will burst out one day, and none can withstand the people's anger. No doubt it has a willing back, but its ears are already pricked and it will not choose men to lead it who would force its hand while kicking its bottom.

Oh, people, poor people, who become king and sometimes even rich, why are your mouths so often open and your hearts so rarely?

VIII

FRANCE AND THE CONSUMER SOCIETY

WAS FRANCE—sorry—I mean, were the French in a sufficiently wretched state on May 1st 1968 to foment a revolution?

I doubt it, though one should not underestimate the number of deprived citizens—solitary, forsaken old people and low-salaried workers, scared to ask for the smallest rise from rapacious bosses. A psychosociologist would perhaps explain how a happy people, or at any rate one of the happier peoples, and the one which is best versed in the art of living, could, through a pathological taste for tiresome problems, have plunged itself unprompted into chaos. Unless an astronomer discovers that this obsessional fever coincided with a sunspot peak and that for lack of a foreign war France had to make do with a civil one.

Since I am no expert in astronomy or neuro-psychiatry, all I can do is wonder whether the French are as dominated by the Consumer Society as some of them claim. This is a newly-invented though not yet patented piece of jargon, so often dinned into M. Taupin's ears that the other day he said to me exasperatedly "I am beginning to wonder whether we were really living before we started to consume".

He is no longer quite certain. Nor am I. But have M. Taupin or M. Jaffredou really become subjects of the Consumer Society, slaves of the C.S., that Minotaur of the atomic era?

I am not sure. At least, not as sure as I would be if we were talking about M. Sven Dagebörd or Mr. Cyrus B. Lippcott. Of course, I do not mean that M. Jaffredou and M. Taupin ignore the call of the new Magi: car, television and refrigerator. But a fierce spirit of independence enables them to escape them much more easily than my friends from Stockholm and Pittsburg. One has only to see how reluctant people are, even in Paris, to graft on an ordinary bathroom, and how, both in provincial and Parisians cafes, the upright stance is still advisable, if not obligatory, in many of those places where only a Foreigner would think of sitting down. The French clearly do not yet worship at the shrine of Saint Sanitaire like those uncouth American, Swedish and even English canonizers who do not recognize the charms of fixed cakes of soap and luminous door-catches.

Like an old sweat showing off to new recruits, I must confess that I have sometimes ventured to bring my small fund of enlightenment to the aid of foreign novices, lost in the dark basements of your City of Light's wonderful bistros. Only yesterday I watched the troubled manoeuvres of a tourist, obviously an American and a man of courage, who had been given a telephone-token but, in the damp, dirty and perplexing gloom did not know which slot to put it in. The acrid emanations made me think of the scent and carnations which the Tourist Board offers American visitors landing at Orly. (I must say it's very curious: you welcome Yankees with flowers; from then on you make sure that their life is no bed of roses; why do you not advise them to keep one of the roses for their subterranean forays?)

So, augmenting your Information Breakdown Service, I went to the aid of this neophyte. I explained to him that in order that there should be light he must first shut himself up in the dark of the call-box, and then fumble around for the latch. Unaccustomed to this method of producing electricity, he was delighted to discover the virtues of the luminous door-catch, brother to the automatic time-switch, and one of those ingenious money-saving inventions with which France is so lavish. He was so delighted that he worked the catch several times. At the fourth go, it developed xenophobia and stuck, and he had to dial his number by the light of his Zippo, which jolly well served him right.

A few minutes later, when extracting myself from another kind of cabin (the kind that the wise man leaves rapidly and backwards if he wants to avoid being caught by the waterspout), I found the American wrestling with one of those miserly taps which dispense a trickle of water on one hand only, and that only with encouragement. The soap resembled a large lemon streaked with blackish veins, and was skewered on a metal spindle attached to the wall. After drying his hands on a rag obviously scheduled as an historic monument, the American surfaced with me. On the way he mentioned the distressing loneliness of the threadlike coat-hanger in his hotel bedroom; and his suffering, too, from the speed with which the phantom tray-hunter who haunts French hotels at a hard-gallop had cleared the breakfast things away.

Were there, he asked, gangs of coat-hanger thieves? Or lunatics whose idea of fun was slipping damp cakes of soap into their pockets? Or Foreigners who tried to cross the frontier charged with Gallic electricity? I disabused him, and he resolved in future to suffer with a smile.

By way of thanks he offered me a drink. When he came to settle his bill, he asked whether service was included.

"The service, yes, but not the tip!" the waiter replied, leaving him in no doubt that France is a mass of delicate shades of meaning.

How can Scandinavian or American barbarians properly appreciate such subtleties? They are brought up without the slightest idea of tipping, and so softened by fluid drives that they find an upright stance inconvenient for certain functions?

Though the globe has become so run-of-the-mill to those robots that they take polar jets as readily as other people take the underground, I am always delighted to find stubborn individualists in your country who refuse to entrust gear-changes to a mechanical brain and do their flying on the ground. Whenever

France and the Consumer Society

Madame Le Vituplet, M. Taupin's cousin 'goes up' to Paris from Carcassonne, she always treats herself to a little trip in a Caravelle at Orly. She goes aboard, the stewardess serves her a grapefruit juice, she shuts her eyes and lets herself be transported to the ends of the earth. But that's as far as it goes. The difference between her plane and Mr. Lippcott's polar one is that Madame Le Vituplet's stays where it is. Air France must have noticed, as I have, that many French people visit Orly in a spirit of scepticism and if they do actually take a plane it is with an expression that suggests it is not really their cup of tea. Air France of course think rather differently. It is nevertheless a typical French attitude, and anything but American. Americans are never so mistrustful; the impression they give is that of believing that the plane was especially made for them, rather as if they had been born inside it.

Naturellement all the French are not made like Madame Le Vituplet, who, by the way keeps a poultice of 150,000 francs on her thigh, day and night. Old francs, of course: it would never occur to her to count in new francs and thus devalue this vital nest-egg, sometimes tucked away in the pocket of her skirt, sometimes concealed in a secret hem, and divided into three 500-franc notes whose numbers have been noted by a notary. "It's safer; you never know."[1]

---

[1] I don't think that there is any relation between this monetary cataplasm and Madame Le Vituplet's longevity, although she is one of those people whose health improves enormously after they have sold their houses while retaining a life interest in them. She has already escorted the first purchaser to the

But there are a lot of people, particularly those approaching the end of their lives, who are as dubious about cheques as they are about planes; who have seen the introduction of telephones and will die without having become entirely accustomed to them; who talk about the 'wireless' and 'gramophone', and don't worry about the difference between a Ferrari and a Peugeot. As I travel through the French countryside I can guess from behind to which generation your inhabitants belong by whether or not they turn round to stare at sports cars.

The habit of using a skirt as a safe seems still to be firmly established. If one could measure the fortune which France conceals in the privacy of its infrastructure (a word much in vogue, which Madame Le Vituplet would not bring herself to use and whose anatomical sense she would no doubt like to see taken out of circulation) the International Monetary Fund would turn round and stare.

But let us ourselves turn round and look at the question of M. Jaffredou and the Consumer Society.

Monsieur Jaffredou is sixty-three, a retired working man referred to by his friends as P'tit Louis. He lives in a little house in Maine-et-Loire, next door to M. de Stumpf-Quichelier, and there he lives quietly,

---

cemetery and the second isn't looking too well. Every lawyer will tell you that this peculiarly French transaction has the effect of reinvigorating the vendor by relieving all anxiety about taxes, insurance and the future, and that more than one title-holder has passed to his last rest ahead of the person whose property he was hoping to acquire with the least possible delay.

guarding his little store of health but not shirking those little tasks which increase his comfort. He does not aspire to greatness, but don't imagine that he hasn't got his own ideas on the subject, for he makes no effort to conceal them either from Madame Jaffredou or from the countryside at large.

In troubled times—during a foreign or a French occupation—it is noticeable that M. Jaffredou never shares his wife's opinions. This form of domestic dispute, which we British would try to keep off the record, is discreetly allowed to leak out and become public property, so the Jaffredous manage to let it be known *sub rosa* that 'they are never in agreement'.

It is a curious fact that in a village where political tension inevitably produces a hail of anonymous letters a household with a reputation for being constantly at war enjoys a special immunity. There is less inclination to hit out at people who are already hitting out at each other. According to the Stumpf-Quicheliers, this kind of third-party insurance dates from the German occupation, during which M. Jeffredou, a Gaullist, and his wife, a supporter of Pétain, escaped reprisals from either side by officially taking it out on each other.

During the course of what you call Recent Events (you seem to have no idea that there may have been others elsewhere in the world) M. Jaffredou, now an anti-Gaullist, kept to the left, while Madame Jaffredou veered to the right. This kept them out of trouble, and their votes should have cancelled each other out in the ballot-boxes. I say 'should have' because, in the light of the figures at Saint-Sornin-sur-Evre, there is reason to believe that a large number of revolutionary voices broke just as they were about to give utterance. (Now I come to think of it, I wonder whether Madame Jaffredou's victory does not symbolize the triumph of womenkind, upholders of law and order and now all-powerful in your country.)

But it was not my intention to ravish the secrets of the Saint-Sornin-sur-Evre ballot-boxes. If I refer to the final voting-figures, it is merely because the mystery itself is illuminating. At least, it is revealing about M. Jaffredou's curious relationship with the Consumer Society.

M. de Stumpf-Quichelier, a member of the middle classes for whom Louis Jaffredou occasionally does odd jobs, tells me that he has watched his working-class neighbour progress in twenty years from a bicycle to a moped, from a moped to a motorcycle, and from this last to a small car, despite the cost of the licence, his teenage daughter's education and the modernization of his kitchenette. (I might mention that though M. Jaffredou owns a cassette transistor, he has not been corrupted by the C.S. to the extent of providing indoor sanitation for his small farm: the outside earth-closet has not been superseded.)

"When you come to reckon it all up," M. de Stumpf-Quichelier remarked to me, "this character, who presumably votes communist, has become more middle-class than me."

"? ?" I enquired.

"His car, my dear Major, the car!"

"*Eh bien*? Yours is better than his, isn't it?"

"Of course, but that's not the point. Suppose I'm up

in my flat and I see a bunch of hooligans setting fire to my car, what do I do?"

"*Sais pas*. You come down."

"Not a bit of it, Major! You think I'm crazy? I stay put. Naturally I'm furious, but I stay put. What's insurance for? And even if I weren't insured, so you think I'd risk my life for a car?"

"*Eh bien?*"

"Well, do you know what Jaffredou said to me when the students began wrecking cars? He said, 'If one of them lays a finger on my bus I'll make mince-meat of him!' And as sure as he's got his hunting rifle hanging up on the coat rack he'd do it, my dear chap, he'd do it!'"

I know all about the Frenchman's attachment to sporting guns but this flabbergasted me. However, I recognized its truth later on: what had affected M. Jaffredou most during the revolutionary disorders was the treatment that the rioters dealt out to cars. And in this respect, he seemed more a victim of the C.S. than Mr. Dagebörd or Mr. Lippcott.

He didn't mind the wings of the Odéon being turned into dormitories and ransacked (Mr. Dagebörd's son might have occupied them, but he would have left them in better condition), the transformation of the Sorbonne into an entrenched camp, the defacing of the frescoes of Puvis de Chavannes, trees being cut down, the students fighting the C.R.S. and treating them as if they were S.S.; nor that, during the rollicking of that bloodstained rampage, certain not altogether studious young women should give the victory sign with their thighs in the Cluny garden—all that could be tolerated, youth must have its fling, and can in any case well do without Puvis de Chavannes. But overturning cars and setting fire to them, that was going too far.

"You must admit," M. Jaffredou said to me, "that they could have done it some other way. Burning cars, indeed!"

Has the freedom to drive become more important in France than freedom of thought? M. de Stumpf-Quichelier believes so and M. Jaffredou proves it. A ruddy-complexioned revolutionary, P'tit Louis sees red if his car is attacked. Does this mean that M. Jaffredou worships it like a goddess and would burn candles to its headlights? Has he unconsciously become a worshipper of the very same C.S. that the revolutionaries blame for everything wrong?

Only up to a certain point, which (so to speak) leaves his engine running in neutral.

Let me try to explain.

To start with, M. Jaffredou is just as much of a weathercock as M. Taupin. If the latter can switch within a fortnight from the rebel's camp to the side of law and order, M. Jaffredou is capable of picnicking on the verge of a dangerous road so that he can gaze fondly at his beloved little rattler, and of taking part the next day in a demonstration against the Consumer Society.

During a general strike, M. Jaffredou is no doubt extremely annoyed that the petrol shortage stops him driving, but not quite as much as Sven Dagebörd and Cyrus B. Lippcott in similar circumstances, for they entirely lack his special private reserves. The inconvenience that he suffers from the absence of petrol, electricity or tobacco is largely compensated for by the secret pleasure that he derives from the knowledge that capitalists (amongst whom, naturally, he numbers M. de Stumpf-Quichelier) are even more inconvenienced than he is.

At the point where a Dane, an American and an Englishman would begin to be annoyed, the sight of Madame de Stumpf-Quichelier going down to the village on a bicycle convinces him that everything is all right. He feels an overwhelming superiority over Foreigners who are slaves to the C.S. He makes remarks like, 'We must take the rough with the smooth, They'll have to tramp it", and "We've lived through worse". What about his car? He can get along without it. Television? He doesn't give a damn. Telephone? Well, it's a blasted nuisance, anyway.

M. Jaffredou is an altruist—his first thought is not for himself. One of his oldest dreams is that everyone should be 'on their toes. As soon as he has said 'They'll have to tramp it' he feels better.

And perhaps this is a key to French character, rather like the one that first opened the gates of French to my astonished ears.

It was three years after the liberation of Paris— brought about as everyone knows (and as schoolchildren are now being taught) by Leclerc's division, and despite Anglo-Saxon opposition. Life had not yet completely returned to normal, and *wagons-lits* were scarce. I had accompanied my translator to the Gare de L'Est, a damnable station from which he had frequently embarked for military service in the dreary barracks at Nancy or Metz, for periods of recall, for Munich and for the war. This time—one swallow does not make a summer—he was going skiing: his children were spending their Christmas holidays in Austria. Two sleeping-cars, fully occupied but with empty corridors, were sandwiched between second and third-class coaches that were filled to bursting: even the connecting gangways were crammed with children and adults. Beside me on the platform was a woman, a mother come to see her son off, who was furious that he had to sit on a suitcase. As the train pulled out she exclaimed:

"Dreadful! People lying in bed while others have to travel standing up! If I had my way I'd make everyone go third class and like it!"

If she had been an American she would certainly have dreamed of a world where everyone could travel by sleeper. But she was French, belonging to a country where a bathroom is still regarded as a luxury.[2] And her dream of making the world as uncomfortable as possible for everyone came as a revelation to me.

My translator has told a number of stories about how my first Notebooks came into being. He has even gone so far as to claim that he himself first conceived the idea, one night when a nightmare reminded him of a Major under whose command he took part in

[2] Even in many blocks of flats in the XVIth Arondissement of Paris and in the suburb of Neuilly it is sometimes difficult to run a hot bath on Saturdays and Sundays, since it is on those two days that the tenants all take their baths. (Possibly actionable note by the Major.)

the retreat from Dunkirk, and who is as like me as a twin brother.

What nonsense. Though I must confess that the Notebooks are to some extent associated with my translator's existence, their real origin is the Gare de L'Est. It was there that a Frenchwoman's remark prompted me to take, if not a season ticket to France, at least a seasonable one.

M. Jaffredou's opinions brought this all-important memory back to me in the most striking fashion.

I wish I could feel absolutely certain that his high hopes of co-management, profit-sharing and the suppression of 'capitalist monopolies' are spurred on solely by a desire to see everyone benefit from a higher standard of living; but there are times when I doubt it.

One such time being when I asked him what his first action would be if the revolution brought him the managing-directorship of M. de Stumpf-Quichelier's or his previous employer's firm.

"To start with, I'd check how much they drew in salary and expenses: chickenfeed it won't be."

"And then?"

"I'd reduce them to the basic minimum wage, same as everyone else, and damn quick about it. That'd get them on their toes."

"What about yourself?"

"Oh, we'd see about that later."

Instead of wanting a lot of people (including himself) to have a better life, would M. Jaffredou really be tempted to start by making sure a few were worse off? I'm afraid I haven't yet found the answer.

But I could not help reflecting, that evening, that the French, who could give anyone lessons in happiness, are never quite at home with money : they always want to appear richer or poorer than they really are. Like the Lyonnais silk-merchants, who only admit to setbacks in their fortunes, M. de Stumpf-Quichelier, who could ride in a Bentley even if he did not wish to show off in a Rolls (what would my workmen think?), disguises his wealth with the anonymity of a black Peugot. He has decreed that, in this lean year, it would be wrong to take off for the Balearic Islands and that his family can very well spend August in Maine-et-Loire. The Jaffredous, who are not rich enough to have such scruples, sent him a postcard from Majorca, occasioning him to wonder once again how the devil they can afford to spend so much.

Could this need to seem—or not to seem—become the most subtle—I was going to say the smartest—adaptation of our old Shakespearean to be or not to be? The English have not got it, no doubt because they cannot grasp it. Faced with a totally incomprehensible play or a canvas so abstract that the painter himself declares that there is nothing to explain, 'because that kind of thing is inexplicable', M. de Stumpf-Quichelier will never look as blank as I do. That he cannot make head or tail of it disturbs his cartesian mind, but does not greatly upset him. What really worries him is that those present may suspect that he does not understand. So while my face remains fixed in despair, he saves his.

And we abandon these intellectual spheres for the street and M. de Stumpf-Quichelier for M. Pochet, the situation is much the same. When a gust of wind blows a Londoner's hat off in the street, his first reaction is to retrieve his hat. M. Pochet's first reaction in such circumstances will be to glance discreetly around to see whether anyone has witnessed his embarrassment.

IX

THE FRENCHMAN'S CALENDAR

 LET US DESCRIBE THINGS as they are, or rather as you would say they are. The 'Movement of March 22nd', which stretched into April to achieve its full flower in May and was 'sanctioned' on June 23rd, made a substantial contribution to my readjustment after so many years' absence. My knowledge of your country would have remained incomplete if your revolutionary days, major events and memorable weeks, deftly slipped into France's already overcharged historical calendar, had not arrived in the nick of time to prop up its foundations.

I know of course that the French have dates in their blood, and that their children learn to find their bearings in the obscure paths of history by means of a series of beacons—732, 1214, 1789—which blink ineradicably in their memories.

It is an incomparable pleasure to watch experienced

drivers rolling, motionless, down the Motorway of History at the wheel of that glorious grand tourer 4-fifteen: 1415, 1515, 1715, 1815, Agincourt succeeded by Marignan, the last rays of the Roi-Soleil gleaming on Waterloo—four hundred years in two seconds—an unbeatable average speed.

I was equally aware that the French keep up the historic garden of their ephemerides—July 14th, November 11th, December 2nd and so on—with such vigilance that January is the only month of the twelve still free to dedicate to a revolution, an armistice or a riot.[1]

I knew, too, that dates like February 6th, May 13th and August 4th act like punched cards on M. Taupin's or M. Pochet's memory banks, causing the appropriate century immediately to pop up in their minds. Each of these figures reminds them of a firing-squad, a change of régime or a night of revolution just as surely as Thanksgiving and Christmas evoke for others the aroma of turkey and plum pudding.

I will not dispute—though it is the fashion to do so nowadays—that 1066[2] means a lot to us. We are even prone, when a tennis player sprains his ankle in the Wimbledon finals, to recall that the same thing happened once before in 1907; all the same, one must admit that the French and a few South American Republics are about the only nations in the world to

---

[1] The 'January Edict', by which Catherine of Medici granted certain concessions to the Protestants, has gradually sunk into oblivion. (Editor.)

[2] William the Conqueror's victory at Hastings. (The Major's note, for the benefit of the French.)

find no incongruity in a street being called rue de 4-Septembre or rue du 29-Juillet. If there is anyone who cannot say which years these dates belong to, it is not because they do not know them but because they have forgotten—there is a delicate difference—it will come back. And God forgive those who are born, live and die in the rue du 4-Septembre without having the slightest idea whether it refers to 1792 or 1870.[3] After all you have people, just as we do, who repeatedly talk of going to Canossa to consult the oracle, and pass away without ever having tried to find out where Canossa was and what actually happened there.

What I did not yet know, what I had failed to learn through never having witnessed it, was the speed with which historic dates ripen under your skies. You have to be as foolish as an Englishman—if you can (for there are certain fields in which our genius is unequalled, leading us, for instance, not even to consider the possibility of an armistice with the Nazis)—to be surprised that such a phenomenon should occur spontaneously in an environment that manufactures instant history. The students of 1968 had not rebelled for more than a week before all the newspapers started talking about the 'Movement of March 22nd' as if it already had a square named after it.

[3] Just to make sure, or for any reader who is in doubt, I will put it on record that : (1) it does not commemorate the massacres of September 4th 1792, but September 4th 1870, the date of the revolution which followed Sedan and overthrew the Second Empire to establish the Third Republic; (2) a Parisian of fifty-five and a bachelor, I have just had to look it up in Larousse. (M. Denainos' note.)

The Frenchman's Calendar

We cannot compete with you on this level, neither in the present or in the past: we have no June the 18th Square to remind us of Waterloo, one of the most glorious days in our history, God knows whether this date will ever have its Place with you . . . But what am I saying? You have thousands of them! For you managed to adopt as your leader someone who, having made a date with history, contrived to establish himself as 'The Man of June 18th' without reminding you for a moment of one of your bloodiest defeats! Marvellous!

But it gets better. The Man of June 18th, spurred on by some occurrence or other, appears on television to appeal to the nation and warn it that the Republic is in danger. The Leader of the Opposition promptly makes a solemn declaration that the voice which has just been heard (on 30th May) "is the voice of the 18th Brumaire, it is the voice of December 2nd, it is the voice of May 13th".

This is of course Double Dutch to a foreign novice like myself. I can only assume that for you it was simultaneously as clear as day and somewhat unspecific, since in one of the most serious newspapers in the universe, appropriately called *Le Monde,* an equally serious expert wrote in an article on the revolutionary days of May: "We shall not easily recover from those nights of August 4th."

Who could have put it better?

If I add that this particular article on the spring disturbances was headed 'A Student Thermidor', and as everyone knows, Thermidor refers to the revolutionary heat of July and August, that about sums it up.

This is something you cannot be beaten at, and our maniacal fondness for precedents, the past and tradition is nowhere compared to yours. One of the most recent proofs is that when we talk about the Normandy landings we never refer to it as June 6th (not even to the man destined to become your President who was so incensed by it), but as D-Day. Is this laziness or a little Yankee influence? I'm sure you can work that out for yourselves.

Still, may I in all modesty point out the threat to France of an overloaded calendar—if not of an overloaded future? Suppose, for instance, one of these strong-arm men for whom you have developed a fondness since you sipped the heady wine of revolution, should seize power on June 18th. Which of the two, he or the General, will take precedence in history as tenant of this date?

Frankly, that's something I would rather let the future decide.

However, if I might retrace my steps for just a moment . . . The rules of common politeness indicate that I should withdraw gracefully, but a respect for objectivity compels me to stay and finish off this brief article with a few observations (once again, all in your astonishing country's favour).

The Italians are popularly supposed to be lazy—and indeed they have barely 2,000 kilometres of motorways. But the French are constructors by nature, and can justly claim to be the greatest bridge builders in the world. No other country can equal them in this respect: France is the only nation to succeed in constructing three bridges[4] in a week, and without working for more than forty-eight hours, and furthermore, making fifty million people cross them. This is no exaggeration: the world witnessed this remarkable achievement only recently. That the country took advantage of Ascension Day to accomplish it does not detract from its worth. The most astonishing part of the whole thing is not the record itself, however— it is that later on it could be beaten.

Saturday bridges, Monday bridges, religious bridges, lay bridges, Saint's Day bridges, national-holiday bridges, bridges in praise of labour, temporary bridges suspended between two permanent ones— every kind comes naturally to the French. Capitulation, liberation, revolution, all end up in France with bridges.

How can Foreigners fail to eye the French with jealousy as they watch them construct their bridges? They know that if they approach them they will find everything closed. What does France care if they flaunt their networks of motorways? She can still pride herself on her bridges, fortified by her good sense, for she is not interested in putting the cart before the horse. After all, without bridges, how can one take advantage of motorways at one's leisure? It is only logical that the Department of Bridges and Highways should neglect the latter because it is so preoccupied with the former.

[4] In France, a working day intervening between a Sunday and a public holiday, and itself taken as an additional holiday, is called a 'bridge'. (Editor.)

But perhaps I shouldn't call it negligence at all. After all those Italian and German motorways, it is a real pleasure to explore the French mini-ways, with their butane-gas picnics, their rural courts, their plain-clothes policemen and the eternal burgeoning of Operation Primavera.

Others may boast of their thousands of kilometres of motorways: France must claim the most artistic, nay the wittiest, road network in the world. The hotel and restaurant signs: 'Le Commerce: its peaceful atmosphere' . . . 'Chez Léon: its paté; and the locality advertisements: 'Embrun, visit its rock' . . . 'Longuy, visit Vauban's ramparts' . . . 'Laon, visit its stairways'; and the customary road signs: 'Beware of soft verge' . . . 'Yellow line unrepaired' . . . 'Road-works for 3 kilometres' . . . 'Diversion' . . . 'Gravel' . . . 'Pedestrian crossing'; one leaps so rapidly from subject to subject that if one wanted to read them all thoroughly one would be constantly melting into the landscape.

While we wait, with M. Pochet, to start melting let us return to the bridges in which the French calendar so excels. A year ago, when I was rhapsodizing about the charms of May in France, which attracts visitors across from all over the world, my translator wrote to me: "You'll see . . . If nothing happens to stop us standing idly by, next year we may well erect a colossal bridge which will take at least a month to cross[5]—a huge structure, flung across the void of May by the Department of Bridges and Highways, allowing the survivors of Easter to plan their summer holidays at their leisure."

[5] Actually forecast in *Figaro* on August 9th 1967. (Editor.)

The Frenchman's Calendar

Incredible! But he was right, and almost to the day.[6] He had not foreseen the revolution, of course—unlike, apparently, all the orators in the National Assembly who, judging by the way they talked about the need for reforms, needed only a gesture, let alone a movement, to start them debating. This is of minor importance, however: the insurrection helped the French to vindicate his prediction, for in the thick of a social upheaval the country showed that its respect for bridges remained intact.[7]

On the Wednesday of the most memorable of all those weeks I met M. Brabanchon. Though the country had already been paralysed by strikes for a fortnight it was in a state of great agitation, the Latin heart of its capital lacerated by riots. The whole nation was hanging on the lips of the oracle, that is to say, on the expected words of its leader, newly returned from Rumania. I took it for granted that the Premier Frenchman (*not* the Premier) would speak early on the following day, Thursday.

"That's what you think!" M. Brabanchon told me. "We may be in the middle of an escalating revolution but that's no reason to skip Ascension Day. We'll cool our heels till Friday naturally. Do you get it, Major?

[6] In May 1968 everything came to a stop for a month. (Editor.)

[7] My translator once recalled in a lecture how, on June 10th 1940, when Paris was on the point of being besieged by the enemy, his superior officer offered to prolong his forty-eight-hour leave by a day because he was due to return to his unit on a public holiday. (Major's note.)

We're supposed to be a secular country! Isn't that funny?"

I should make it clear at this point that M. Brabanchon, although apparently anti-clerical, is a practising Catholic (when he chooses to be); and that while he maintains a suitably middle-class opposition to excessive personal power, this does not prevent him from being all for law and order when it comes to cutting down trees. In short, he is a Frenchman; a real one, whom the French provoke to 'mild amusement', which is to say, 'grinding his teeth'. When M. Brabanchon says "They make me laugh!", you can bet your bottom dollar that he has never been more serious.

As you can imagine, I have as much trouble finding my bearings in M. Brabanchon's private calendar as I do amid France's historical caprices.[8] I never quite know what to make of him. As he was saying when I so rudely interrupted him:

"Frankly, Major, they are absolutely killing! Look,

[8] But bear in mind that France's *climatic* calendar is just as confusing. Tourists find themselves engaged in a perpetual game of hide-and-seek with the seasons. I thought my translator was exaggerating when in one of his books he wrote that the right season always came immediately or a few days after the time you have chosen. "How silly!" I said to myself. "He has to make things up to have something to write about." But I must admit that, if I do go south in September there is always someone to regret that I did not come when the mimosa was flowering; and I almost always arrive in Normandy to be met with laments that the apple blossom is over. I say 'almost' because once I did get there at the right moment. Whereupon M. Taupin promptly said to me, shivering, "It's too early for Normandy: you should have waited till July."

a young and more or less stateless Jew triggered off the workers' uprising, and they've forbidden him re-entry into France. And, at the same time, they keep us hanging about till Friday as if we were run by the Vatican! And for what? To honour the memory of *another* Jew—not to be compared with the first, naturally, but just as much of a revolutionary . . ."

A month later M. Brabanchon voted for de Gaulle and took advantage of a bridge hastily thrown up between two others to add two days to his holidays by leaving on a Friday evening; thus demonstrating the wiliness of the French, who do not start their holidays for forty-eight hours after they themselves have started out.

It is clear, then, that though they sometimes grumble about bridges both M. Brabanchon and M. Pochet are all in favour of one that comes at the right moment, and even try to lengthen it. I even know some people who left proudly for a long weekend and still haven't come back. Mark you, nowadays people are so constantly on the move that it's a shock to find them at home at all. "Aren't you taking advantage of the bridge?", we say, as if they were avoiding a patriotic duty. Family men in good jobs are perhaps the least serious-minded—what am I saying?—the most con-scientious of all: in addition to the ordinary school holidays, they tack on business trips, conventions and relaxing weekends. It would be quite wrong to imagine that people like that ever take holidays. It is a word that their secretaries never use: their employers are always 'away', 'in the provinces', 'abroad', 'out of town' or 'travelling'—never on holiday. How exhausting for them!

And dangerous, too. Millions of drivers cross these bridges, and it's only too well known what they cost France in dead and injured.

That is why I am greatly surprised that no observer, sociologist or statistician has ever, to my knowledge, stressed one of the outstanding results of the recent revolutionary occurrences: namely, that in 1968 France was saved from a great massacre by a little insurrection.

Has sufficient attention been given to what would have happened if a bunch of students with a questionable sense of responsibility—but certainly responsible for one of the most serious social upheavals in France for thirty-two years—had not, as you say nowadays, 'triggered off the escalating process' by 'starting off the dialogue' with an irreverent kick up the backside of the establishment?

Instead of four dead and three thousand injured, France, peaceful France (by which I mean that part, working-class or promoted entrepreneurs, which goes to war on the roads every Saturday) would no doubt have mourned the 450 dead and 11,500 injured that the five weekends of spring usually cost her on that highway battlefield.[9]

In fact those wild young revolutionaries can never be thanked enough for their sudden initiative; while allowing the communist trade unions, the Christian

[9] In the merry month of May 1967, the weekend dead and injured were 433 and 11,572. The *total* dead and injured for the month came to 961 and 26,792.

trade unions and other demonstrators to jump on their band wagon (a vehicle mentioned in no timetable) they created a petrol shortage and so prevented people driving to their deaths. George Bernard Shaw once regretted that youth was wasted on the young. This episode proves him wrong. America, Germany, Italy and even Great Britain, all deplore the numberless senseless deaths each week; they would profit much by following the example of the French people. Always clever at puns, they could have shown you better than anyone else that conversations prevent conflagrations.

And their Minister for Tourism could justifiably have continued his publicity abroad, despite the free-for-all:

'Visit insurrectionary France! The only country in the world to suffer fewer deaths during a revolution than in normal times!'

This was proved as soon as peace was restored to the community: a few hours after the day of the 'de-escalation'—as it happened it was Whit Monday—the roads were again strewn with dead and injured.

For France is a lover of processions: she defies the damned and damning statistics, and does not draw back from any bridge. Wheel to wheel, steeled against collisions and determined not to yield an inch of ground to attackers, she hurls herself fearlessly into battle. No doubt everyone thinks himself protected by a good spirit: it is of course the same spirit that hard-working France puts into the building of her bridges.

X

MOBILIZATION DOES NOT MEAN WAR

 SHALL I ONE DAY take my courage in both hands and hurl myself into this struggle all alone, like a grown-up? Should I seek to take my place in that intrepid band, without the protection of the St. Christopher which M. Pochet keeps attached to his dashboard? For this patron saint seems to be undergoing a motorized decline and these days is appreciably slowing down.

Grand Dieu![1] I am not at all sure.

Frankly, it is not a question of courage. The risks do not bother me a lot. What I lack is the vocabulary and the skills of making war in peacetime.

This is yet another field in which we cannot compete with you. We have always been taught never to speak of our successful exploits and to keep quiet about other people's, and I have always wondered how we

[1] "Good Lord!"

manage to weather the ordeal of conversation. It is probably thanks to the weather. But this is not the immediate problem, and though the world is eager to find easy explanations for everything, far be it from me to hurry to settle one of its few undecided questions.

But to return to the matter in hand. . . . I should point out that *we* only wear our decorations in civilian life when we are formally requested to do so on cards inviting us to receptions. Once the war has been cleared away, we do not like either to recall its ups and downs—however gallant our conduct may have been —or to chew it over again. This distinguishes us from some Frenchmen who, having finished with the war, eat it. The shells of Verdun still cheer up confectioners in that martyred town and indicate, in chocolate, a curious difference in our tastes. Although we are very fond of sweet things, it would never occur to a pastry-cook in our country to offer his customers Trafalgar cannon-balls of nougat or a Scapa Flow toffee torpedo. This is due, no doubt, to lack of imagination, or perhaps simply insensitivity in a people whose silences, I must admit, can be confusing. A short while ago, during a cocktail party at a house in Shropshire where I was staying, a young Frenchman on holiday explained to a benevolent-looking man of fifty how he had thrown a tear-gas grenade back at his assailants in the Boulevard Saint-Michel in 1968. Judging by the attention that the venerable gentleman paid him for twenty minutes without asking for the slightest reciprocity, the young man was hardly to guess that he was talking to an R.A.F. veteran with a D.S.O. that he'd picked up stooging around Berlin air-space on seventeen extremely unhealthy occasions. You have to be English to fool people like that so quietly.

When, talking about bridges, I spoke of not ceding an inch of ground. I must unconsciously have been obeying the strange martial law of your country.

I have never been in any doubt that France is a harmless dove, and ought to be constantly on her guard, she is a soft victim, lain in wait for by fierce enemies or torn asunder by the dissensions of her own citizens. How should I doubt it when you are continually saying it or writing it? It would be most unsporting to doubt your word. But I am still learning, *de visu* and *de auditu*, that your most pacific euphoria resounded with military strains.

The Great Exodus Has Started...Warning Systems Improved...40,000 Specials Mobilized For Great Summer Offensive...Open-Air Court-Martials For Suspects...

Historians interested in this *fin de siècle* will no doubt record that in the sixties, dawn of the civilization of leisure, the western bridgehead was temporarily reprieved from the apocalypse and gradually began to apply war phraseology to holidays.

Each August, as it comes round, assumes a martial guise, and H-Day becomes D-Day.

But newspapers, radio and television do not wait for that dreaded day to warn the country of its imminent danger: as early as the end of June they start to point out the precautions to be taken to avoid encirclement, blockade and disaster. July approaches, and national tension increases moment by moment. A state of emergency is declared. Control of weapons is set in motion. Specialist troops—gamekeepers, motor-cycle and plainclothes police—urgently recalled to the colours, are already at their posts, ready to take command of the millions of happy new recruits, the army of holidaymakers.

Then, after several feverish days, comes general mobilization, announced, if not by *tricolore* posters, at least by headlines: 31 MILLION SOLDIERS PRE-PARE TO KILL TIME IN HOLIDAYS. The date more or less coincides with that of the Ems telegram on the Sarajevo incident: between July 13th and August 4th. This time, admittedly, mobilization does not mean war, but it is none the less general. TWO MILLION PARISIANS FLEE THE CAPITAL de-clare the papers, as though Paris were threatened by a siege or a gas attack. The railway stations are taken by storm and fighting breaks out. The first communiqués are signed by the S.N.C.F., and one day, when the civilization of leisure has its textbooks, school children will learn that on August 1st 1966, fifty-two years after the start of the conflict that was to return Alsace and Lorraine to France, Parisian railwaymen entrained the whole population of Strasbourg—229,000 people —in one day. There is talk of 'the second battle of Austerlitz' and 'the taxis of the Marne'. "*J'offre*", the famous General, crops up again[2]—"les meilleures

[2] General Joffre was of course a great French hero of the Great War.

garanties de sécurité,"[3] says the S.N.C.F. "Travel by train!"

Certainly air travel, safe as it is, carries certain risks. The greatest confusion reigns at Orly, where numerous skirmishes have been reported between French troops, called up to join their units on the Cote d'Azur, and foreign fifth-columnists who have been parachuted into enemy territory, and claim priority. *Ils ne passeront pas*! The difficulties experienced by first-aid air-hostesses in separating the combatants are increased by the latter's tendency to take advantage of the situation and become rather too friendly. The first wounded are attended to in hospitals (invariably 'improvised', because of the French talent for improvisation). While the trains, albeit overloaded, carry the troops to their destinations, thousands of airlifted holidaymakers, arriving at Nice airport one August 2nd, take a full hour to cover the 5 kilometres separating the airport from the town, and half a day—in some cases a whole day—to flee the invaded city and reach their camps by the shore or in the countryside.

On the roads there is a free-for-all. Fifty thousand motorists are trying to escape—but in vain. M. Pochet, who has a logical mind, had promised me that if we set out on a Monday we should avoid the crazy mob that had rushed off on the Sunday; but, he was not the only one to come up with an original idea, for everyone else had had it as well. However, what with the cunning people who are not afraid to leave on a Sun-

[3] "I offer the best guarantees of safety."

day just because a lot of fools want to avoid the crowds, and the shrewd Monday travellers who are silly enough not to do the same as other people, a miraculous balance occurs without any contrivance, and the numbers on the road are about the same on both days. It is enough to drive Pochet mad with rage, if he were not in that state already. Don't talk to him about staggered holidays! His holidays are nicely staggered, along an 18 kilometre queue which will remain stationary for an hour, pointing towards a south it may never reach. His rage is transferred to his foot, which jams the accelerator down on the floor, or to his hand, tooting his ill temper to the world at large: a world made in his image, thousands of Pochets, Taupins and Turlots, motorized troops furiously marking time in their metal carapaces bristling with underwater guns, nautical skis, spades and tent-pegs. They have put a tiger in their tanks; they roar but they fail to spring.

However, despite the apparently desperate situation, good humour has its champions: the unquenchable life-and-souls-of-the-party to be found in all troop movements shout "To Berlin!" and "To Cannes!" with equal enthusiasm but with the same note of revenge, and their *Chant du Départ* resounds through the countryside. A few peasants abandon their tractors and come to the side of the road to gaze at these townspeople disguised as rustics, chat to them and thus seal the holy alliance. M. Pochet, whom these charades remind of certain departures from the Gare de L'Est in the direction of the Vosges,[4] has no heart

[4] Departures for the front.

for such merriment. On this first day of jollity he is in pretty bad shape. On edge like everyone else, he takes it out of his wife, who-has-never-been-able-to-read-a-map, on his children, who-should-have-done-it-before-they-started, and on everyone who does not know how to drive. Though England is in no way superior to you in this field, he begs me to forgive his country, which is 'the absolute bottom' when it comes to motorways. He had expected to do at least a furious 60 kilometres an hour: he is furious because he has only done 25. It's ruined his average, it's completely messed up his holiday and his engine is boiling over. What on earth has got into people that they should all choose to leave at the same time? The world must have gone stark staring mad. Everyone except him, that is; he is a family man, unlike all these gigolos, and has perfectly good reasons for setting out on August 1st.

Having decided to stop for lunch before lunchtime, in order to make some progress while others will be lunching, Monsieur Pochet chooses a two-star restaurant where he gets a dirty look from the headwaiter when the children order *oeufs en gelée* and coca-cola. This cold repast does not stop the bill from heating him up.

Burning from being cheated—though not for the last time—Pochet sets off again, angrier than ever to find the road just as congested as before. Trying to alter the clock was useless; other people had thought of it too. Maddening! Once again he becomes a sheep, bleating away with his horn at helmeted shepherds, or proceeding by little leaps and bounds. At six o'clock that morning, after a preliminary struggle with unruly suitcases, he had said, "There's not a moment to lose!" Now, whole hours speed by while we speed not at all. To kill them, Pochet switches on the radio: expecting to be distracted from his troubles, he learns from a reliable, if sinister, source that in the last forty-eight hours 167 of his fellow-creatures have met their deaths on the holiday front, that the injured total 4,831, and that before the day is over the roads will account for a further 125 deaths. Why not include him while they are at it? that would finish it off nicely! The statistician, expanding his necrological announcement, goes on to estimate that in ten years road deaths will compete with Hiroshima.

M. Pochet shudders, develops a fit of the shakes and narrowly escapes a collision which would have helped to make that damned forecast come true.

Once again he is off to war, this time against the Ministry of Works, which exercises its ingenuity by starting to dig the road at the worst possible moment; against the police, who slow down the traffic just for the hell of it; against the insects, which choose to crush themselves directly in his line of sight; against the dotted yellow lines, which exasperate him so much that he can no longer follow them; against holiday-wars; and against war-holidays.

I cannot sufficiently emphasize the courage, the coolness and the self-control required at these moments of stress to resist making an about turn and heading back towards the exquisite calm of one's abandoned hearth. It is true, of course, that an about turn is virtually impossible, as well as against the regulations. One-way roads have been introduced to canalize the exodus. Any backward move would be doomed to failure, and giving ground would threaten the backslider with death from collision with the descending flood, or render him liable to heavy penalties.

For the forces of law and order are on the alert. Operation Overlord has been succeeded by Operation Holidays. Watched by 20,000 policemen, 14,000 gendarmes and 7,000 C.R.S. and motorcycle police, who keep a close eye on them and often make them pay dear for it, spied on by patrol cars, ambushed by speed-traps and overflown by helicopters, any complacency on the part of the refractory is premature. But some people cannot resist temptation, in spite of rural courts which permanently sit throughout the countryside, concealed from the army of holidaymakers by an ingenious camouflage of bushes or fruittrees. Summarily convicted by a swift courtmartial, the guerilla convicted of taking a bite out of a yellow line while overtaking at an unsuitable moment, is subjected—sometimes with the whole district watching him on television—to the humiliation of a breath-test, the torture of the locked wheel, the shame of suspension. The roadside disciplinary powers first compel him to restore bit by bit the fragments of yellow line weighing on his conscience, then snatch away his driver's licence and strip him of his movable property. It is a shaming capitulation in open country, an appalling degradation which reduces the rebel then and there from the status of wealth and authority to that of an impoverished, deprived pedestrian, soon to be directed with his arms and impedimenta to the nearest railway station and there picked up by the iron hand of the S.N.C.F.

Thus discipline, which gives armies their strength and ordinary folk their weakness, keeps M. Pochet clamped to the wheel of his car and ensures that he should prefer remaining in the field to the ignominious penalties of the alternative.

He had lovingly concocted an itinerary, consisting of long pieces of red roads, little mouthfuls of departments and succulent titbits of three-star restaurants. But all his plans were thwarted. He was seized by a longing to chuck the whole thing and go home by train like a common defaulter. But, no, he pulls himself together—duty comes first.

Encircled, watched and followed, Monsieur Pochet becomes obsessed by the yellow line. In the end it hypnotizes him as a boa constrictor fascinates its prey. He stops worrying about being overheard by enemy ears: for now plainclothes policemen are spying on him. Who knows whether the man in a polo-shirt whom he is about to overtake, and whose innocent-looking car, loaded with fishing-nets and children's spades, so closely resembles his own, is not a counterfeit Pochet, part of the police fifth column scattered through the ranks of genuine combatants? Battle-shocked, his nerves in a tangle, haunted by fears of breaking the law and on the verge of breaking a blood-vessel, he overtakes in terror, reduces speed in a panic and even as he prepares to prostrate himself before the God of Gendarmes and denounce his neighbour, he hears a voice barking at him, as if he were back in barracks, "I don't wish to know that!"

For only the roadhog who has just scorched past him ever gets pardoned—one of those roadhogs you come across everywhere and, naturally, never catch up with again. Just as it is extremely difficult to unearth an ex-Hitlerite in Germany, it is almost impossible to find a roadhog in France, or, rather, to meet him outside of items in the newspapers. Have you ever heard anyone say "I'm a roadhog"? Certainly not. One sees roadhogs on the road, of course; but once they reach their destination they are neither visible nor recognizable, since the tares of speed become mixed with the wheat of caution. The roadhog disguises himself as a benevolent parent, pats his children's cheeks and quietly becomes indistinguishable from the fifty million good Frenchmen.

By the time we finally reach our goal in the middle of the night, the dirty dog will have arrived and be tucked up in bed and sleeping the sleep of the just. Stiff legged and as dead-beat as his little family, Pochet still finds the strength to smile as he gets out of the car: "We beat them hollow, Major!"

A nice hot bath. A nice little dinner. A nice sleep. And life will be beautiful again.

The small hotel (category: simple but comfortable) stolidly awaits us, with its haggard night-porter and two shutters that rattle in time with Pochet's knock.

Would it be possible to make an exception and serve a light supper in the bedroom? "The children are so ti . . ."

"Now, monsieur? You can't be serious! Supposing everyone began asking for that! Besides, the cook went off hours ago."

Well, sleeping is as good as eating. Dazed, Pochet goes upstairs, his family in tow. They had been promised No. 26, view of the sea. They are given No. 54, overlooking the railway.

"We don't have many trains," says the porter. "The first is at 04.20. The second at 06.10. I sometimes wonder why they bother to have a line at all. Besides, it won't be for long. No. 26 will be leaving in two days: the children had measles. We could hardly throw them out in the street."

Not at all worried by this state of affairs, the porter adds, as he shows them into No. 54. "Means you won't have to bother to unpack tonight."

No. 54 has two cage-like cots and two beds for adults jammed into a parallelepiped; it reminds Pochet of a barrack-room.

Never mind. He will camp. Me too. *A la guerre comme à la guerre!* One does not really need so much. Just a bath. No. 54, being on the railway-side, does not have a bath. Well, you can't have everything. And anyway there is a bathroom on the same floor. "You'll have it all to yourself at this hour." The water is tepid. I wait. Then I try again: it runs cold. I ring. No one answers. I ring again. The porter is very tough, he does not find the water as cold as all that. And in any case it is no longer running.

"Of course. Everyone runs his bath at the same time, before dinner. No wonder there's no hot water left. The best time is in the morning about six before they all get at it. Then you'll be able to have as much as you want: and it'll be boiling, too!"

This simple-but-comfortable hotel would do better to call itself comfortable-but-simple. Never mind. We will wash tomorrow. We will eat tomorrow. We will unpack tomorrow. A good night's sleep and all will be forgotten. The porter was right in advising us not to unpack: we would not have known where to put our things. There is one pitchpine cupboard, one door creaks and the other refuses to open, two coat-hangers dangle carelessly, as if they were just hanging around for the ride.

Pochet cages the children and goes to bed, the road in his legs, the railway at the back of his head. Perhaps the miserable condition of the coat-hangers has affected him, he decides that anyone who chooses to go on holiday in August must be wooden-headed. Twenty-seven million wooden-heads would make, at a conservative estimate, ninety million hangers. Having worked this out, he falls asleep and dreams of coat-racks. No surprisingly, he clings to them and brings down the crossbar. As he falls into a bottomless cupboard, a car driven by another roadhog without lights crashes into the door. Pochet wakes up in a muck-sweat. It's the train ... It's the car ... It's the coat-rack ...

"The children!" he yells.

No. 53 knocks on the wall. No. 55 is shouting. Pochet wants to switch on the light. Instead, he rings the bell.

It's always the same story with those pear-shaped things: one never knows whether one is going to switch on the housemaid or ring the electric light. Neither responds. France is a niggling country, preoccupied with mechanical pears. Pochet falls asleep again. This time he dreams of pears.

Some dawns sing. This one yells. Is it the children in No. 53 or the 6.10 train? It's the kid in No. 55, whose first cuff of the day has coincided with the whistle of the 6.10 express, which unfortunately caught his father unawares. You can't expect the walls to be soundproof in a 'simple' hotel like this. You can hear everything until the train goes past and then you can't hear anything at all.

Breakfast is frugal, the coffee as thin as the walls and the butter almost as invisible as under the Occupation, despite being wrapped in silver paper. All this must be carefully worked out to suit the incredible speed with which the housemaid arrives to remove the tray.

I accompany the Pochet's to the beach. In contrast to the luxury hotels, which have a *plage privé*—sorry, *un beach*—the 'simple' hotel is situated far enough from the sea for reaching it to give one a sense of triumph. And, after all, if you do not see it by day, at least you do not hear it at night.

"We won't take the car," M. Pochet tells his children. "Come on, we'll walk! One, two! One, two! There's nothing like a good walk at a good pace in

good fresh air before a good bathe—unless you'd prefer a good box on the ear?"

Rebuffed like pariahs from the entrances to several
private beaches, we finally reach the shore proper, to
which access is just as strictly controlled.

"Have you got your beach-card?" a life-guard dryly
asks a dripping M. Pochet. "No? Then you must re-
gister at once."

M. Pochet duly becomes a member of the beach.
His card entitles him to all the privileges of a full
member, and in particular the right to be on the sand
—or what remains of it, at least.

Pochet was not far from the mark when he was reminded of the Occupation. Typical of the half-dozen
departments to which France withdraws and almost
swamps in the summer, Ravanel-sur-Mer is full to
bursting-point. The August influx has raised its population in two nights from 200 souls to 15,000 bodies.
Faced by this invasion, the natives put up a strong resistance, defend their territory foot by foot and, far
from being drowned themselves, drown the invaders
in an incomprehensible jargon.

The beach is black with brown people, though
patches of sand are just visible here and there amid
the various tans. Picking their way over prostrate
bodies, beachcomber Pochet and his beachcomber
wife, followed by their small dolphins, now members
of a club of the same name, manage to stake a claim
to four square yards of unoccupied territory.

A thousand kilometres away from the impossible
parking-meters of Paris, Pochet now finds himself
parked by the sand-metre. Expecting to escape noise

and traffic-jams, he is now trapped in an inextricable congestion of bodies and subjected to the torture of compulsory transistor radios. He hoped to forget the crowds in the underground, but now he meets them again in what the brochures call 'delightful surroundings.' He longed to forget all about time and to live without making plans or appointments, and he is now forced to book half an hour on a tennis court, a week ahead, to queue up for a stamp, an ice cream and a shower, and to answer 'Present!' at the physical culture sessions on the beach. He has reached the position of departmental manager in an important firm, the ruler of twenty-five employees who would not dream of taking the slightest liberty, and now he finds himself being scolded like a child by a P.T. instructor who taps his middle-aged spread in front of two hundred people and tells him, "We'll have to get rid of that!" then gives him a regimental number, 403B, and orders him to fall in at the end of row C. Having fled Paris in search of the sun, he is now compelled to flee that heavenly body at the best moment of the day, when there is a chance of expanding his few metres of sand, in order to avoid paying dearly for the lunch, announced by clanging bells, which is included in the full pension that his barracks (hotel) insists on him taking.

This, then, is how M. Pochet spends his holidays. The end of August will come as an immense relief; so much so that he will find himself thinking, as he did at Lunéville, 'Escape at last!' He will count himself lucky if he reaches home in one piece, a survivor from the ebb-tide that sweeps the sun-jaded soldiers back towards Paris.

XI

OLD SEX IN THE NEW SOCIETY

You put up barricades without producing a revolution, and you are still talking about it.

We have produced a revolution without putting up barricades, and we seldom talk about it at all.

We must, of course, agree on the nature of this revolution. More often than not, when Frenchmen speak of our 'social revolution' (a somewhat over-worked expression) they mean the same old frigid, naval and corseted Britannia disguised as a dolly-girl, concealing her nudity under a transparent raincoat in a Kingdom reduced to the boundaries of Carnaby Street.

Simplement insipide!

I could hardly ignore the extremely disturbing spectacle which the Mother-city of the Empire today offers the bulging eyes of an ex-Indian Army Major, returning to the fold after fifteen years abroad.... If it is

true that General de Gaulle, seeking the ultimate revenge for the Burghers of Calais, wanted England to
appear naked at the gates of the Common Market, we
are on what I might hesitantly call the right track.
Nowadays our young women reveal to all and sundry
what in the past was difficult enough to get a glimpse
of even in the privacy of the bedroom, and which, in
the case of my dear first wife, Ursula, now deceased,
it took me three months to unveil (God rest her soul,
if not her body). When I think of the advice which
her mother gave her on the eve of her wedding—"My
dear, I know it's disgusting. But do what I did with
your father: shut your eyes and think of England"—
I can scarcely believe I am still on the same planet.

However, I must face the fact that I am. And, despite my overstimulated reflexes, I am determined to
keep a cool head. Undoubtedly times have changed
since the arch-Victorian Lady Plunkett and her
friends modestly draped the legs of their grand pianos
in muslin. *Et alors?* Young Englishwomen may ex-
pose themselves—when they are sitting down at least
—'up to their marriage'[1]; our venerated *Times* may
decide, after 182 years of reflection, publicly to remove its long chemise of small ads and exhibit the
bosom of its news[2]; but it is still possible to find in the

[1] This is not one of *our* expressions. It emanates from a little
French girl, precocious enough, or in any case, sufficiently well-
informed to know that something important occurs in that
area. (The Major's note.)

[2] What cheek! But the strip-tease has stopped short there,
and there is no reason to believe that it will go any further
before 2784. (The Major's note.)

green depths of Sussex and Somerset austere scholastic establishments which possess no mirrors, and where nudity is prohibited, and where the worthy heiresses of a stubborn aristocracy wear combinations when taking their baths and are only allowed to go for walks—in straw hats with chinstraps—in pairs (changing their companions daily).

What does all this mean?

It is very simple: everything has changed and nothing has completely disappeared. If it takes something of everything to make a world, we can find everything it takes to make the kind of world we want to see.

Puritan Albion and Swinging England are not as badly matched as some people claim: they quarrel, inevitably, and may reach the brink of a legal separation, but no divorce will follow. There is in fact a tacit and mysterious understanding between them, the reasons for which, as we shall see later, are somewhat confused.

A new, uninhibited generation, so uninhibited that it sometimes gives vent to its feelings with bicycle-chains, openly ridicules the army and goes so far as to dance to 'God save the swing'. But how do they dress, these daring young people who denounce the hideousness of school uniforms? In uniforms: teenagers in tight, buttoned-up tunics; young women in long coats of navy-blue cloth or red cité resembling the formal get-up of Grenadier Guards—a form of dress that the strictest governess would never have dreamed of imposing on her charges in the Bois de Boulogne even in the days when her word was still law. The Victorian choker, apparently unbearable, now reappears and is worn with the greatest pleasure.

The scholastic establishments previously referred to, hardy survivors from old-time strictness, have never succeeded in smothering the volcanic temperament of our girls. The truth is that supposedly prudish Albion lived for more than a century with a totally false reputation. The nation of Henry VIII has always been one of the bawdiest in the world. It is useless to impose on it the corset of Victorian puritanism—whalebone always snaps sooner or later.

The good burghers of Calais or Paris who send us their children each summer to improve their English should always remember that the time is not long past when any traveller from the Continent of the slightest importance, when he visited one of our cotton-mills, was offered the prettiest of the winders as a matter of courtesy.

Thus nine times out of ten it is in our cottages that your boys lose their virginity—at the same time, let it be said, acquiring a good accent, thanks to the affectionate creatures of Kent or Surrey who co-operate in their initiation. I shall certainly not be contradicted by my friend and translator, P.-C. Daninos, who, after repeatedly warning his son about certain men of this realm, subsequently learned that though his offspring had gone astray, in the neighbourhood of Canterbury, he had nevertheless erred in the right direction.

We are a strange, princely-socialist Kingdom,[3] as

[3] Perhaps we should remind our reader that in this Kingdom where a public school is, in fact, private, an 'affair' does not mean a profit, in shares, it is a matter of love. . . .

rich in paradoxes as your own monarchist Republic....

One day sociologists studying this era may perhaps
realize that barely forty years before the year 2000,
members of Her Gracious Majesty's Parliament were
capable simultaneously of voting in favour of the aboli-
tion of corporal punishment in schools, and of deplor-
ing its disappearance in the Press—particularly in
those papers that owe their brightest (or shadiest) success to detailed accounts of flagellation parties in
baronets' Tudor castles.[4]

And capable too, of seeing that homosexuality is
made legal, if not actually noble, by the House of
Lords which sent Oscar Wilde to prison, while at the
same time closing the Royal Enclosure at Ascot to a
divorcé, whether Prince or pansy.

As for the legend of swinging England or even
swinging London, it is in danger of becoming as non-
sensical as that of Gay Paree—both of them the invention of damned Foreigners. It was magazine editors
in Paris, Milan and Bonn who led the stampede to
stereotype our 'social revolution' in its spiciest aspects
by instructing their reporters to: "Dig up something
really swinging about swinging London.... What's
'in' and what's 'out' ... know what I mean?"

Of course these days you can easily spend a week in

[4] Not a day goes by without the papers announcing that
teachers, parents and even pupils have joined forces to demand
the return of corporal punishment; or without *The Times* or
the *Daily Mail* publishing a nostalgic letter from a retired Major
or an Old Harrovian declaring that a good hiding never did
anyone any harm.

London without seeing the least scrap of English thigh. It depends, among other things, on your choice of district. To catch England by its long hair and short skirts you could not do better, or at least have done a few months ago, than visit Chelsea or the West End.

And today? Today the supposedly swinging miniskirt, which has become so short that it doesn't swing effectively, is withdrawing to the provinces, its powers of provocation neutralized by a monstrous regiment of midis.[5] Having only just accustomed myself to the idea that I had seen everything (or at least almost everything) I find myself being shocked to the core of my Major's soul by the realization that in concealment, so much can be exposed.

I am sorry to have to say that the truth lies elsewhere and, at the risk of disappointing the French, that it must be sought not beneath our skirts but, as you say, in our structures, or to be precise our trade unions. Not very sexy and considerably less enticing, it nevertheless deserves an eight-column headline:

ENGLAND HAS CHANGED SOVEREIGNS

The headline is accurate enough but to the best of my knowledge no sensational weekly has ever printed it, and I tremble at the thought of being the first to do so.

There has certainly been a 'social revolution', but the real revolution, without a capital R or capital punishment, is the one which without displacing the

[5] No doubt it will prove difficult to explain to the French what is particularly Provencal about a skirt of that or any other particular length.

Queen from Buckingham Palace has placed the all-powerful unions on an invisible throne. The benevolent tyranny of the Establishment has surrendered to the dictatorship of trade unions, without whose approval nothing can be done, not even—as M. Pochet observed in a London hotel—the replacement of a burnt-out electric light bulb by a waiter.

On this occasion the waiter politely explained to him that he could not deal with that kind of thing without getting into trouble with the electricians' union, which is itself divided into seven or eight sub-unions according to the voltage or specialities of its members. So M. Pochet had to wait for a union electrician to arrive.

But this, after all, is a matter of minor importance. I know of a car manufacturer who triggered off a strike in his factory by reducing from twelve to eight the number of highly skilled specialist teams engaged in distributing tea to the workers on the production line. And manufacturers will sometimes stop the line altogether if a workman catches cold rather than face all the bargaining with haughty unions which the provision of a temporary replacement entails.

As there is always something true in the false and every mendacious assertion contains an element of truth, I am going to make a shameful and disgusting admission: the real revolution, as far as I am concerned, the one which curdles my military blood, is the phoney one.

Dare I confess it (hypocritical method of indicating full intention of doing so)?

Only fifteen years ago, when some devilish chance

bent my steps towards one of those Charing Cross Road Bookshops of ill repute, crammed with 'French books' exclusively made in England. Surreptitiously glancing around me to make certain there was no one I knew to remark my presence in such an evil place, I bought the *Kamasutra* and stuffed it into the pocket of my raincoat.

Today I can peacefully leaf through *A Study of the Use of the Whip by the Victorian Disciples of Sacher-Masoch* or *Sexual Behaviour of the British Female* in the front of one of those shady shops without anyone taking the slightest notice. And why stop there? I could hold the *Lexicon of Erotic Sex Potions* in one hand, and in the other one of our little mini-skirted Red Riding Hoods, all ready to be devoured by a big, bad wolf of an ex-Indian Army Major, and no one would mind.

Only a short time ago, shifty-eyed individuals would shift rapidly away—as I would have done myself—with *Lady Chatterley's Lover* in their mackintosh pockets. The same people, or their sons, now buy the *Encyclopaedia of Eroticism* as openly as if it were *The Jungle Book*. And why should they make a secret of it in a world where omnipresent sex is flaunted everywhere? Those questionable photographs that shady hawkers still offer at night in the streets of Pigalle, shuffling their packs of salacious cards under their coats, here become *tableaux vivants* played in the nude in full daylight. In certain sections of the King's Road, young things of sixteen display so many of their attractions that even in bed there would be no more surprises. Our most secret inclinations, the ones the ragging and promiscuity in public schools used so dangerously to develop—and still do—are advertised in neon lights. But on the day I felt my personal revolution was complete a Soho cinema a stone's throw away from the Charing Cross Road announced in letters of fire: *THE TORTURED FEMALE*.

Below, in much smaller letters, a poster qualified, 'For members only'; but it was abundantly clear that anyone with the price of admission would be allowed into this murky establishment. At a nearby news-stand I was tempted to buy, for a few shillings less, a copy of one of our most distinguished women's magazines, 'Queen'—very popular with men, *naturellement*. Conforming with the fashion for sulky looks which seem to have invaded the cover-girl world, it displayed over six glossy pages a nymphet in an ultra short nightdress and high, white, laced boots, playing the part of a little girl being punished under the stern eye of a servant in a starched cap—Nanny, '68 vintage—grasping a rod which only just perceptibly ended as a feather-duster.

Should we complain, or merely recognize that we are now doing openly what our forebears did in secret? I asked myself this question a short while ago as, accompanied this time by my translator, I again strolled down Charing Cross Road, casting what I hoped was a casual glance into the windows of those satanic bookshops.

Plexus, Sexus, Sadism, Fetishism, Masochism, Variations in Sexual Behaviour, Guide to Sexology, Kamasutra, Erotikon, Sexual Behaviour of the British Bachelor—everywhere sex, challenging, provocative, aggressive and just dying to keep the British bachelor company. I found myself unable to resist.

After only a moment's hesitation I approached one of the shop assistants. "Excuse me," I said, "This is a French friend of mine who hasn't been to England for a long time. He'd like to know how long you've had that revolving stand there, with all those books on it."

"I should think it'd be about five years now," the man told us. "We must have put it in when we were allowed to sell *Lady Chatterley* . . . Now, here's a book you ought to read: you'll find it very interesting."

He handed me a slim volume entitled *Sexual Customs of the French*, remarking with a smile at my friend, "Of course you won't need it, sir!"

He was quite wrong as it turned out. Daninos confessed to me later that he had learnt a lot from reading *Les Habitudes Sexuelles des Français*: there were at least two *habitudes* that he'd never heard of.

XII

FRENCH RESTRUCTURED

WHAT A LONG TIME AGO it seems that the only thing the French broached was their good wine! Today, if they broach anything, it will be the subject of the future gloomy, civilization facing a crisis, the hazards of fate, dictatorship, restructuring, a still immature Europe.

C'est terrifiant!

Fifteen years . . . a tiny grain of sand in the hour-glass of evolution, yet what radical changes—sorry, I mean *mutations non negligeables*—have occurred in that infinitesimal space of time! I would never have dared to talk about *sole promotionelle* in my first Note-books like your favourite housewife on *telex consommateur*, or *discussion sectionelle*. I was then at the foot of my educational climb, busy struggling with phrases which mean almost the exact opposite of what one

would expect, like *faire long feu*[1] and *coupes sombres*[2].
I am a man accustomed to saying brigadier when I
mean *general,* umbrella when I mean *parapluie* and
terrace when I mean almost anything except a *terrasse*[3]; I am therefore the last person to reproach you
with corrupting the foreign invader by forcing your
vocabulary on him: we are the experts in this field,
and we have a lot more words than you. All the same,
you must admit that you can put up a strong defence,
and that to grasp certain nuances used in the best
society—"He may be a silly bastard, but he's no fool "[4]
—one must (as you say) get up early in the morning.

I have always done so, as a matter of fact, in the
hope of getting to know you better, but frankly that
last subtlety is beyond me. And I am afraid that all
my efforts to speak and write French correctly, ham-
pered in any case from the start by my habit of mumb-
ling and an appalling accent—will come to nothing,
since the little bit of French that has stayed with me
seems old-fashioned and unsuitable for human con-
sumption.

How the devil am I going to find my way?

When I last left you, not so long ago, your only
platforms were at the back of the Paris buses: I used
to love to cling to the handrails and be gently rocked

[1] Literally, 'to fire a long way'; actually, 'to hang fire'.
[2] Literally, 'dark cuttings'; actually, 'slight thinning' (of a
forest).
[3] In French, *Brigadier* is a police-sergeant; an *ombrelle* is a
parasol; and a *terrasse* is the stretch of pavement in front of a
cafe.
[4] *"Il est con, d'accord—mais il n'est pas bête."*

across the capital as if I were on the bridge of a ship. Alas, they have almost disappeared from the R.A.T.P.[5] and now enrich the language of politicians and trade unionists; instead of allowing me to glide backwards to a soft landing on the pavement, they serve as a foundation for party programmes or to have demands launched from them.

Fifteen years.... Is that all? Your taxis were old but not yet all of a *conventionnels*. The situation was not always good; nevertheless it did not *se dégrader*. And how did you manage to argue so much without a word of "initiating a dialogue"? Though your statesmen, like ours, 'explored new horizons', they could not —since at that time they lacked 'variable geometry' planes—take a *survol de l'actualité*.[6] Perhaps, for that reason, they received fewer unpleasant surprises ... still, you've made a lot of progress!

In those recent times you explained; you did not make explicit. You had your motives; not your motivations. If he wanted to make an appointment with me, M. de Stumpf-Quichelier took out his *agenda*; he did not know the giddy pleasure of consulting his *calandrier*. I could park my car, but parking meters had not yet materialized. A footballer merely played a good game; he was not in a position to command an astronomical transfer-fee. A young tennis champion tried to live up to the high hopes that people had placed in him—but how would he have set about fulfilling his contract? And I have recently learned from a Biarritz beach-superintendent on T.V. that all

[5] The Paris Transport Board.

[6] Literally fly over (i.e. review) current events.

those deaths from drowning on the treacherous shores of the south-west which you used to deplore were simply due to the inadequate infrastructure of your beaches.

You used to go on holiday without being holiday-makers. You went out in pleasure boats without being pleasure seekers. And if your politicians took timely advantage of a situation, they were not opportunists.

The famous D system was in full swing, but you had not yet found a way of applying it literally: I had never before met: demythify, demystify, de-escalate, depassionalize and even deceiling—quite apart from those that I could not understand at all. Your Minister of Education talks of 'departitioning secondary schools' as if he were referring to the septate nostrils of a rhinoceros. And one of your Police Commissioners went so far as to declare that it is essential to "de-crystallize parasitic parking', which 'sterilizes the roadways with blood-sucking cars'.

I suspect, though I am still not quite sure, that this supercharged language is all part of a vertiginous toppling into technical terminology. In those primitive times, hair driers were not yet telescopic, soap-powder biological, meat deep-frozen, flour extra-proteinized nor vacuum-cleaners high-powered, nor were your defences all in the azimuth.

In a nutshell, the context was born but was not yet speaking. I do not know whether one should look for additional reasons, but it is clear that you were still living in an era of underdeveloped language when a mackerel[7] had not yet become a promoter and pigs,

[7] *Maquereau* means both a mackerel and a ponce.

poor creatures, would have been unable to exercise an option.

Exaggeration? *Nenni*,[8] as you would no longer dream of saying. For I have in front of me irrefutable proof. Option, the modern word for choice; option, which one would look for in vain in the works of Voltaire or even Valéry; option, which Louis XIV would have chuckled over—while that monarch undoubtedly governed France without the benefit of structures or fork lifts, one may well wonder how France managed to get along without them from Charlemagne to Clemenceau—options have finally reached your countryside. It was of course foreseeable that the deluge of options with which politicians, trade unionists, technocrats and pedagogues overwhelmed it, would eventually leave it without a choice. In the important daily paper *Ouest-France*, under the headline 'Our Soil' I read in an article about a cattle-breeders' convention:

"The Western white pig has reached a stage in its career when it must take up options which will decide its future for the next decade."

I must confess that my first reaction was one of pride. Pride for you, as if I were already one of you. How could one fail to be proud of a country where pigs have reached that stage of progress where they have options between one truffle and another open to them?

Nothing would seem to establish more firmly the rule of Her Majesty the Option, only yesterday a prerogative of technocrats and politicians, than this farm-

[8] A charming dialect form of 'no', like the English 'nay'.

yard promotion. At the same time, one cannot help regretting that this choice lady should be walking the street, letting herself be taken advantage of by unscrupulous people who commit the same crimes against her as they did her elder sister, Alternative.

I was driving with M. Taupin the other evening when we happened to switch on the radio in the middle of one of those discussions about some topic of the day during which members of the audience can speak on the telephone to celebrities. The first voice I heard was that of a young man, who gave his age as twenty-five and went on to say, "There seem to me to be two options. . . ."

It does not need second sight to guess that this lad had recently been presented to H.M. Option and had not yet learnt how to handle her. When he said two options he meant two possible solutions or one alternative, so that this was a case of 1 + 1. Never mind. . . . In these days of rising verbal prices, an option or two makes no odds.

What was the problem that so perplexed this young man, apparently reared on National Administration School milk—or on the Political Science feeding-bottle? Was it a question of political ethics? Of his career? Of family-planning? Not at all—he was talking about a trip to Canada:

"Either I can go on an organized tour, in which case I can leave everything to the guide; but won't I be losing my autonomy? (*sic*) . . . Or I can go on my own, but isn't that rather risky, and won't I risk missing something that way, too?"

What a terrible dilemma! And all because of that

damned option! When I think that nowadays Social
Security, Europ-Assistance or Preservatrice-Loisirs
offer the daring traveller insurance of every kind,
covering anything from the breaking of spectacles in
a common or garden bus to the fracture of a tibia in
the mountains (provided at least that the insured has
not ventured off the beaten tracks stipulated in the
policy), a trip that I dared to take all by myself at
the age of eighteen, and which included travelling
steerage from Southampton to the Piraeus, now seems
to have been bristling with dangers. I am glad to know
that these hazards can now be insured against and that
young people can safely travel with their eyes closed,
protected by their comprehensive policies. All the
same my spirit of independence is aroused and I hope
that, as I write these lines (without any assurance that
they will be published or paid for), our Optional Uly-
sses will have plumped for the more perilous alternative.

If I have mentioned these three minutes of radio
time, it is because they prove how much the supercharged vocabulary of modern technology benefits
your young people, right from their first halting
words.[9] And I cannot contain my admiration that so
many lips, trained in recitation from a tender age and

---

[9] And our adults, too, it would seem, judging from a brochure
issued by a firm of management consultants. 'The search for
and selection of executives', it reads, 'is entrusted to specialists
uniquely capable of studying the post to be filled, and defining
the optimum profile of the man who should fill it.' To be an
executive is already something, but if you've got an optimum
profile as well, the whole thing is a piece of cake.

in an atmosphere of innocent curls, simple frocks and flat shoes, should so readily come out with 'optional', 'sectorial' and 'infrastructure'.

As I try to fly unaided in your new sky of words, the breaking of the sound barrier seems to present more difficulties every day.

I had another proof of this only yesterday, in the branch of the Société Générale where I keep my account (you will observe, by the way, that of all the banks available I chose the one whose name recalls the leader to whom I have sworn allegiance). I asked for M. Ballandois, whom I usually deal with.

"M. Ballandois?" said one of his colleagues, "I'm sorry, he's at Barbizon being recycled."

I hope I shall be forgiven—and believed—when I say that this immediately summoned up an image of M. Ballandois in shorts, pedalling away behind a trainer in the forest of Fontainebleau. However I was mistaken. It was explained to me that M. Ballandois was not staying in Barbizon to ride a bicycle or have a breath of fresh air, but to undergo one of those mutations peculiar to this era of technical metamorphoses, in a hotel converted into a training centre. M. Ballandois was, in fact, sloughing his skin, and it was a question of 'giving him a scent'—as you have been saying for some time in your orderly language—of the new terminology, as applied to long-term loans, foreign imports, the provision of credits for French exporters and the financing of foreign contracts. In short, he was being 'alphabetized'[10] by the re-education of his automatic language reflexes: he was recharging his batteries by disconnecting his consciousness.[11]

I was flabbergasted for a moment, as though paralysed on the edge of a seemingly impenetrable jungle, in which the birds no longer spoke the language that I expected of them. But, though M. Ballandois's recycling riveted me to the spot at first, it swiftly filled me with new determination: if a Frenchman of thirty-three, assistant manager in a branch of the Société Générale and well thought of by his superiors in the hierarchy, needed to be recycled in one of your beautiful seminarized forests, how much more imperative was my own reconversion!

I immediately decided therefore to leave for another, equally romantic glade[12] for an initiation course in 'General Semantics'. (You must admit that the first of these two words is always cropping up, sometimes as an adjective, sometimes as a noun, in your titles: *secrétaire général, administration générale, président-directeur général*—France is devoted to the General. Specializing in the recycling of the average man, 'the General Semantics course (employing a non-Aristotelian methodology) teaches the student to see more clearly, more quickly and further', and no messing about: it offers A NEW ATTITUDE TOWARDS HUMAN AFFAIRS (I was unaware that, for a man, there were alternatives, but it was just what I needed).

[10] *alphabetize* is not, of course, susceptible to translation. (Editor.)

[11] I'm getting the hang of it, don't you think? (The Major.)

[12] Louveciennes.

So I am being initiated into the mysteries of intentional and extensional definitions, I try to avoid 'over-partial habitual perceptions' and 'rigidity of categorization', and I am sure to distrust 'signal reactions'. And there is no need for me to feel submerged by all these terms, for General Semantics, undertaking my defence against 'abusive grammar', is there to save me from deception by 'the mirage of words'. How? By seeking their 'signification, not in the words themselves but in the person using them (principle of multi-ordinality)'. Any chances of success are especially good because the basic works of the founder of 'General Semantics', Korzybski, are written, as his name would suggest, in English,[13] and have not yet been translated.

Louveciennes is definitely a place for foreigners. And I have no grounds for complaint. For, though M. Taupin sometimes declares that he cannot make head or tail of present-day French, I am picking up some English.

I am compelled at this point to admit that Anglo-Saxons go out of their way to complicate matters and have aimed some below-the-belt blows at your beautiful language although it is already hard pressed by technical jargon.

At first I attributed it all to your love of paradox. The French, I told myself, are unique! Their guide, a Perrichon on an international scale, crosses the road to avoid greeting the Duke of Edinburgh; the G.I.s are suddenly in disgrace and swiftly sent back out of the country they surreptitiously entered in 1944; the

[13] *Science and Sanity, Manhood or Humanity.* (Editor's note.)

Government neglects to send a representative to the remembrance service at Vimy for the 60,000 Canadians who, *pour vos beaux yeux,* closed their own eyes for ever; an insidious anti-American wind is allowed to blow throughout the country on the pretext that the American way of life mortally endangers the Latin Genius—all this at the very moment when the French decide without rhyme or reason to Americanize themselves.

Perhaps I should have said Anglo-Saxonize themselves, for, ignoring drugstores, have they not installed a 'pub'— yes, the 'Churchill Arms'—within a stone's throw of the Etoile? And am I not sometimes compelled to walk three kilometres to find one of your charming columner urinals, now heading for extinction?

No! All that was too beautiful, too ugly, too extravagant to be true, or at least to be natural. There was something shady about it. And I suspected that subversive foreigners had a hand in it. If a managing director like M. de Stumpf-Quichelier chooses to mix Anglo-Saxon words into his vocabulary until it becomes a sort of cocktail—*"Ce matin j'ai fait du* brainstorming *pour le lancement d'automne . . . C'est très utile. A propos vous savez que James est devenu un très bon adviser? J'ai comme un petit feeling qu'il ira loin."*—well, if it makes life any easier, good luck to him. But I find it extraordinary that a whole nation should spontaneously come to prefer *le living* to *la salle de séjour, le job* to *la situation, l'impact* to *l'incidence* and *l'attaché-case* to *la mallette;*

that it should fall for *les gadgets* and be tempted by *rotissoires multicook, cuisinières jetgaz* or *lessives au dermasoft*; that it should allow its children to work out their complexes in *blue-jeans, style campus*, become increasingly devoted to *le relax en polo-shirt* and put up as many electric fir-trees for Christmas in Paris as there are in Manhattan. Only someone who didn't know much about the French would imagine that they descended this fatal slope of their own accord; as if it could be any part of their real make-up to take a fancy to *les posters, les badges, les hit parades, le show-business, les twin-sets, le whisky* or (what am I saying?) *Byrrh on the rocks*! Clearly they were forced into it. Could you have borrowed so much from the Americans, who are after all children at heart and a trifle primitive round the edges, and the hypocritical Anglo-Saxons, because you feel some lack? Of course not! Only some hidden force could induce you to imitate their *magazines* to *faire du shopping, du nervous breakdown, du planning* and *du marketing*.

A thorough investigation has convinced me that the American Secret Service is behind it all. Only an organization of that kind could compel you to swallow the commonplace words of strip-cartoons, so that you pass *les tests* and resort to *les drugstores* instead of to your own cafés. To explore the subject in even greater depth I went to see Colonel Donovan B. Curtis, one of the top men in the American Persuasion Forces. Head of the Nylon network which has trapped France in its mesh, he became famous by persuading two Frenchmen, Jean-Philippe Smet and Claude Moine, to call themselves Johnny Hallyday and Eddie Mitchell. *Intolerable*!

"I must admit," the Colonel told me, "that, in their case, we were assisted by a very active fifth column."

He went on to disclose that the next U.S. offensive would be based on super-astringents, though this, in fact, would only be a diversion. The hexagon would be attacked in much greater strength by a fresh wave of strip-cartoons, computer commandos and regiments of copying-machines (for copying French inventions, naturally). Troops—a battalion of cover-girls—were already standing by to give covering fire.

"We have already contaminated 75 per cent of French products," the Colonel told me, handing me copies of your newspapers, pullulating with polluted advertisements: *'After-shave'* toilet-water, *'O' Yes'* brassières, *'Exciting'* suspender-belts, *'Daffodil'* poplins, *'Slim-line'* dresses, etc. "The only resistance left comes from the Marquise de Sévigné[14] and your noble vintages. But your glorious Benedictine has already engaged John Fatsbury of the University of Syracuse to handle its publicity, and your Chartreuse advertisements talk about *'les drink'*.

I should have suspected as much: there will always be collaborators. I had yet another proof of this the other evening at Orly. A Frenchman was seeing a foreigner off on his plane— *un jet* or *un Boeing*, no doubt. As he said goodbye, he called out "Don't worry about coming back, old chap! You'll always be welcome, whatever they say!"

[14] A make of chocolates.

French Restructured

He said it like a man who is not afraid to speak his thoughts out loud. In bygone days he might have been addressing a hereditary enemy. But, as you will have guessed, on this occasion it was to an American that that Frenchman was saying goodbye.

XIII

YOU ARE MARVELLOUS

 WHETHER HEAD OF STATE, vox-pop man in the street, or egghead expert, television has compelled men to submit to its laws and increased their natural tendency to 'do a turn'. I am beginning to wonder whether in these days of interstellar rockets we are not also living in an era of hawkers.

Royal hawkers, sports-hawkers, trade-union hawkers, news hawkers—every kind flourishes in this atomic, flashy century, when princes, suddenly endowed with ubiquity, make door-to-door calls on fifty million individuals at once, drop in to the Pochet's dining room to talk to them *en famille* about France's affairs and, through the scintillating talents of a magic box, manage to make the most refractory nation as good as gold.

It was only to be expected that an invention of this kind should increase tenfold the Frenchman's opportunity to display his talent for acting—a realization that first occurred to me one evening when France, locked in a sitting position and hanging on to every word that the oracle uttered, was listening to the President of the Republic tell her fortune.

Once again the orator bowed to the rites of the screen. Condemned for the moment to solitary confinement, wearing make-up, his glowing eyes emitting Jovian flashes of lightning, this all-powerful man was none the less the slave of the Goddess. His astonishing memory, his ability to arrange complex ideas into a logical sequence without the aid of notes and his magnetism made him into a real Telepresident. Like certain actors, he had a 'presence'—and one which he was ready to prolong. In the course of half a century I have seen three French Presidents whom the Goddess would ruthlessly have eliminated because of some physical defect or marked lack of charisma. But this one was a first-class author-actor-producer. He proved it that evening by showing himself to be in turn a master of suspense (for seventy-five seconds France was left wondering whether after placing himself at the wheel he was going to let her bowl along on her own); an excellent salesman (if you do not adopt my methods you will run into a lot of trouble, even if you use my subsidiaries); a wheedler ("You know me very well, after all we have accomplished together"); a traditional orator, skilled in the use of political jargon and the language of an old campaigner (France 'heading towards the abyss', while of course 'the whole world', having nothing better to do, looks on in delight); an arch-persuader ("I hope ... I believe ... I KNOW—

147

with a wink worthy of Mounet-Sully—that you will back me up.") Nineteen out of twenty. Not quite so good, perhaps, as one of his impersonators, but who would deny the profound influence that a mere actor's gramophone-record had on the diction of a President of the Republic? No more sibilancy, no more tremulous *"naturellements"*, nothing to provoke more criticism—or another gramophone record.

How far down the ladder must we go to see this great art practised more or less felicitously?

Eh bien . . . everyone does his 'turn' whatever way he can—news items, disasters, athletic records, heart transplants. Everyone adds a little of himself to each event and fills his audience with contemplation, hilarity or indignation. A psychiatrist would no doubt say that there is a transference, a transference induced by the commentator who describes the funeral of a Head of State as if he were Bossuet delivering a funeral oration; by the compère of a televized quiz-game who, having embarrassed one of the competitors by asking him the name of the ogival arch parallel to the axis of the nave, announces, glancing at a slip of paper, that it is the wall rib, as if the word were as familiar to him as the alphabet; by the demure *speakerine* who, landed with the weather forecast, adopts the mood of the elements, playfully announcing sunny spells, and solemnly warning of 'atmospheric disturbances leading to rainstorms, which will gradually become widespread over the whole country', like a sympathetic bringer of bad news.

You Are Marvellous

This is another part of my project that I find particularly troublesome: Suppose that one day I should prove worthy to become one of you; I have observed for so long the strict neutrality of the B.B.C. and Radio-Lausanne in the atmospheric field, how can I change now? It is true, of course, that my accent will always prevent my being offered this kind of job. This is just as well: I should never dare to emulate your young lady and endow the sun with movement of an intimate, personal nature: "After rising at 4.59, the sun will refuse to go to rest before 20.56."[1]

In the same way, I shall never acquire the skill of your news-reader, who takes equal advantage of good weather and bad to link up one topic with another.[2] Is the sky blue? "Well now, on this sunny Sunday we must try to give the sunniest news we can. . . ." Is the forecast gloomy? Then the announcer will amuse himself by extending the inclemency of the weather to politics: a storm is brewing in Czechoslovakia, the situation remains cloudy in Vietnam, a chilly atmosphere hangs over the Common Market and a tempest is raging in Biafra.

Every turn of events, furthermore, must have its music or its theme-song. In the field of news, the back-

---

[1] As you say, '*sic*.' But nothing between the inverted, however, unlikely, commas is invented.

[2] In its French form the art of transition is constantly reaching new heights in this medium. At the end of the television news, I heard the Stock Exchange man take advantage of the last sports shot (of a weightlifter lifting nearly 400 lbs.) by announcing that "French securities could well do with a dumbbell expert to keep prices up".

ground music must fit the picture as subtly as the commentary. Thus there is catastrophic music for floods in the U.S.A.; frenzied music for the fair in Seville; solemn music for the black marchers in Alabama; and dramatic music for the war in Vietnam. All these types of music must, I imagine, be kept in filing cabinets (Carnivals, Cataclysms, Combats), and I am surprised that there are not more mix-ups. Jolly or tragic, the music fades out and the commentator fades in, also in a tone of voice appropriate to the occasion; and he seems incapable of changing the subject without suitably smoothing the transition: "Now, with your permission, I am afraid we are going to turn to a much more serious matter. . . ."

Uncivilized English and American reporters still follow the powerful, coarse formula of Where? When? and How? but the French, having reached the peak of civilization, can never allow the news to emerge naked and alone. They dress her up. Not having any of those chicken which must not be counted too soon in the absence of confirmatory news, or those invisible dancing shoes suitable for a subject that prudence demands be approached on tiptoe, he usually covers her nakedness with a prefatory "Well. . . ." For instance, instead of simply saying, "Soviet troops moved into Czechoslovakia last night at 0.37", he will start off, taking pains to look as grave as the situation, "Well, it's happened! The Czech spring has suddenly given way to Soviet winter . . ."—an elegant preamble adorning a gaunt headline, and one which would earn his Anglo-Saxon counterparts the sack on the spot.

This manner of dressing up the news can end with

disguising it altogether, as when a commentator instinctively introduces France into an event in which she took no part. For example, the Soviet Premier and the President of the United States meet at Glassborough. It is clear that France had no part in the meeting whatsoever. But on his way home Mr. Kosygin, passing through Paris, pays a courtesy visit on the President of the Republic. The commentator, giving this a personal gloss, says: "Mr. Kosygin has been to see General de Gaulle to report on his recent talks with President Johnson."

Though this somewhat nationalistic transference of the commentator's secret desires to the facts of the news constitutes some kind of a record, all records are beaten when it comes to the world of sport. Did I say 'beaten'? I should have said 'pulverized'. For, in this era of superlatives, there is no more beating, only pulverization.

It is high time that someone demolished the myth that the English are kings in the realm of sport. You have become much better than us.

To begin with, our commentators are complete nonentities alongside yours. One needs tremendous experience of important tennis championships to call out on T.V., after a double fault by an Australian in the Wimbledon finals, "No, no, my dear man! You don't serve that way!", or after a muffed passing shot, "You may be thinking like a fox, but you're playing like a carthorse!" No English commentator would dream of adopting such a patronizing attitude, unless perhaps he himself had once been a finalist in the world championship—and to the best of my knowledge we do not possess such a phenomenon.

But *you* do. And in every kind of sport. In the European swimming championships at Utrecht, your T.V. commentator showed marked signs of exhaustion: "Be careful! *We've* still got 400 metres to go!" One could have sworn that he was doing a telecrawl alongside the French team. At the finish, he managed to gasp out, "Our heart was in our mouth. We're still trembling!" And take cycling—your men are always there at the Tour de France, pedalling away in the first person plural, like the sports reporter who publicly exclaimed, "Biquet, old man, why on earth couldn't you have changed your tyre like everybody else? You wasted seven whole minutes—an agony that we shared with you, nom *d'une bicyclette*."

I came across your tireless and ubiquitous reporters again in Grenoble at the Winter Olympics where, judging from their commentaries—"She's doing very nicely" . . . "Not bad at all!"—I realized they must all have been former champions. And listening a little later to pathetic panting from a certain king of the microphone who lost his voice in the middle of a hockey match, I began to wonder which was the more meritorious, the herald or the hockey-players, and whether, amid the avalanche of medals awarded to France, there might not be one for him.

And even for Pochet: by the end of those memorable games, where the French medals shone with such brilliance that even the bronze ones eclipsed the Foreigners' golds,[3] he seemed surrounded by a halo. Who could deny that he too took part?

Once again I must apologize. If I ever said that the French were less sporting than us, I take it all back. I never realized that a whole country could become a nation of champions in a mere ten years, and so easily —or, as you say, in an armchair. Not long ago, to be labelled a sportsman (by the newspapers, at least) you had to be agile enough at least to secure, possibly by force, a place in the open air in a grandstand at Longchamp or Colombes. Today, thanks to the universal amplification of television the tens of thousands of 'sportsmen' have become ten of millions. One cannot deny that sport has made progress in depth, even if the depth is only that of a sofa.

All France runs with Jazy's legs, does the crawl with Claude Mondonnaud, turns on its back with 'Kiki' Caron, sweeps down the Andes with Périllat, climbs the Galibier with Poulidor, dribbles with Kopa, goes over the sticks with Jonquères d'Oriola and clings to the Dru with the rescuers from Chamonix.

An exaggeration? I asked Pochet one day whether he would be free on the following Saturday, he answered, "I'm afraid not. I've got France-Scotland at three o'clock."

The best proof that he plays an active part in the game when he leaves home to watch a match is that he is congratulated on his performance. "The specta-

[3] After one race the commentator dwelt for a long time on Annie Famose's achievement in coming in third and winning a bronze medal and then referred much more briefly to the Canadian Nancy Greene, who, "I should add, won the gold".

tors weren't just good : they were wonderful!" a T.V.
commentator once declared at the end of a match—
and I know of a travel agency which, to attract a public used to being insured against everything from birth,
is thinking of issuing a special 'sportsman's ticket' for
the next Olympics (wine included, and a rebate of 10
per cent if France fails to win any gold medals).

Meanwhile Grenoble has given Pochet his revenge
for the humiliations suffered at Tokyo, for though he
is perfectly prepared to invent any number of excuses
to get his daughter off gym, he found it quite intolerable that France required the co-operation of a horse
to carry off a gold medal at the Olympics. And there
still echoes in his memory the commentator's lament
over the Japanese short-circuits to which the French
fencers fell victim in the electric foils : "Three geishas
are coming forward to present their medals to the
winners. They are wearing kimonos in iridescent colours. How much more iridescent they would seem to
us if our medal were a gold one!"

So it is not going too far to say that, when the Government decided to decorate Killy with the Légion
d'Honneur, the whole of France felt herself decorated
at the same time. Pochet, his legs still shaking after
the vertiginous descent, could scarcely conceal his
pride. The Premier made no attempt at all to conceal
his. "I am proud of him," he said, like Napoleon talking about one of his Old Guard. Exercising transference on a national scale, the Head of Government
went on to declare, "When a nation is at the top of
its form, it is reflected in every field!"

And with a passing but well-directed thrust at us

he added that 'the passionate will to win which was until recently the prerogative of the English' was now inspiring the French. What a difference between present-day France and that of 'forty years of languor!' Clearly the failure of the French to pull their weight in the Olympic Games was due to the weakening effect of party games.

I could not fail to be convinced by these statements,[4] if only in retrospect. If a French team managed to win the Davis Cup in 1927, despite the slackness of the Third Republic, it was because her "Musketeers" had foreseen, though omitting to mention it to anyone, the coming of the Fifth. Their 'passionate will to win' was prophetic.

Whether they are congratulating Killy on being the fastest Frenchman downhill, though he is actually of Irish descent, their voiceless colleague on having overcome his disability to the greater glory of hockey, their runners for giving their all or their women for looking so pretty alongside the track; the female champions for kindly coming to the microphone despite their exhaustion; or the sun for joining the party, if not the patrie—your T.V. commentators are simply participating in a rite that has been magnified by the little screen; that of self-satisfaction.

From your erstwhile Leader, who always found something to congratulate himself, right down to the most inconsiderable quiz competitor, being congratulated on placing Rio de Janeiro in Brazil and not in

[4] Made to *L'Equipe,* a sports publication.

the Argentine, the whole nation runs on applause as a lorry runs on diesel oil.

A man with a sack of sand on his back covers fifty yards without falling on his face: "Give him a big hand: you don't see that too often! Well done!" France is beaten by the All Blacks: "Well played, All Blacks, but well played, France, too!" The ambulance brigade displays its talents: "Well done, ambulance brigade!" A motor-cyclist delivers a film in time for the performance: "Well done, delivery boys! Bravo, France!"

The number of things on which you can congratulate yourselves is quite extraordinary. The President of the Republic congratulates himself on so many journalists turning up to hear him speak. The municipalities congratulate themselves on being able to welcome the President of the Republic. The reporters congratulate the municipalities on the welcome they have managed to provide. At the end of August, I heard a television news-reader congratulate those of the French people *who were still on holiday*. I even heard a candidate running for deputy congratulate someone on being an Auvergnat—and the Auvergnat congratulate himself on being one. Since I started asking myself "How can one be French?" the little box has taught me, better than years of coexistence have done, how well the "How can one be Persian?" side of you still flourishes. An illustration of this was given on T.V. by the French owner of a flat in Spain, who found 'the sea and the sun very agreeable and the people very pleasant; but their mealtimes and their shops . . . are utterly impossible'. He went on to say, "What's more, there's no way of getting them to alter them. WE WILL JUST HAVE TO GET USED TO THEM!"

I don't think one ought to be as Spanish as all that!

And when you are not congratulating, you are thanking. For nothing, for everything, for any old thing; by Christian name, by surname, in the name of the French people. A distinguished sports-commentator was heard to thank a rugby player on the screen. "In the name of French sportsmanship, my dear Paul, thank you! One mustn't be shy of putting it into words: you played a splendid game!" If there is no champion—or star of some other kind—to thank, they thank each other. "Thank you, my dear Maurice, for that brilliant commentary!" When a racing expert arrives, puffing and blowing, at the top of the grand-stand at Longchamp—"from which I have the honour of greeting you"—to give a commentary on the Grand Prix, it is already no mean feat; there is something in his struggle for breath that reminds one of Borotra in his palmy days, and one is on the point of going to his assistance when a colleague lends him a helping hand: "Ah, thank you, my dear Victor, for kindly giving me the odds!" He makes this service sound so invaluable that I thought for a moment he was going to thank Victor in the name of the whole nation. The start of the race is announced: the commentator thanks the cameraman (by his full name) for kindly focusing his camera on the objects of the commentary; the horses, whom he congratulates on their speed, or a fashionable woman, whom he congratulates, in an aside, on her elegance: "Thank you, dear lady, you look lovely!"

Finally, he will thank the winning owner for kindly saying a few words over the microphone, and congratulate him on having managed to make his way through such a dense crowd.

England is supposed to be a polite country, but television has never thanked me there as it has in France. In your country I am thanked the whole time: for being there, for staying there, for my attention, for kindly giving it, and for continuing to give it 'to the very end'. And, as if that were not enough, I am wished a good lunch, a good afternoon and a good weekend. You could spend a whole year going on like that. It seems that it is only with the greatest difficulty that the announcer can tear himself away from me, and I understand much better now how the French have spent nearly a hundred out of the last two thousand years just saying goodbye on their doorsteps. The goodbyes range from "Madame, Monsieur, Mademoiselle, thank you for your kind attention, good-night!" to "Thank you for your kind attention. All that there remains for me to do is to wish you a pleasant evening, a pleasant night, and a pleasant Sunday: good-night and thank you!"

I could swear that this bespectacled guardian angel, telewatching over France, will come to my hotel last thing at night to tuck me in. It really is too kind of him.

You can say it again—you really *are* wonderful! The impossible does not exist in France! France quite amazes England! But now I must leave you. Goodbye and thank you. Thank you for having come all this way. Thank you *infiniment*! *Merci* very much!